HOW SOON IS
SOON?

OTHER BOOKS BY MARVIN MOORE

The 144,000 and the Nearness of Christ's Return
The Antichrist and the New World Order (also printed in Spanish)
Armageddon: The Devil's Payday
The Case for the Investigative Judgment
Challenges to the Remnant (also printed in Spanish)
The Close of Probation
The Coming Global Crisis
The Coming Great Calamity
Conquering High Mountains
Conquering the Dragon Within
Could It Really Happen? (also printed in Spanish)
The Crisis of the End Time (also printed in Spanish)
The Delay
Discoveries in Partnership
Forever His
The Final Crisis
The Gospel Vs. Legalism
How to Come to Jesus (also printed in Spanish)
How to Grow in Jesus (also printed in Spanish)
How to Handle Competition
How to Handle Fatigue
How to Handle Guilt
How to Handle Your Imagination
How to Make a Decision
How to Prepare for the Coming Global Crisis
How to Think About the End Time
The Invitation (32-page magazine)
Is This Living?
The Long Road to Armageddon
Prescription for Reconciliation
The Refiner's Fire
Sacrifice
Straight Thinking in the Age of Exotic Beliefs
Television and the Christian Home
What Happens When You Die?
When Religion Doesn't Work
Where Is Bobby Now?
Witnesses Through Trial
Yet Will I Serve Him

HOW SOON IS
SOON?

MARVIN MOORE

Pacific Press®
Publishing Association
Nampa, Idaho | www.pacificpress.com

Cover design: Daniel Anéz
Cover art resources: GettyImages.com
Interior design: Aaron Troia

The author assumes full responsibility for the accuracy of all facts and quotations
as cited in this book.

Additional copies of this book are available for purchase by calling toll-free
1-800-765-6955 or by visiting AdventistBookCenter.com.

ISBN 978-0-8163-6814-3

January 2022

CONTENTS

Foreword: A Tribute to Marvin Moore   7

Introduction   9

Chapter 1:   Abraham's Expectation   11

Chapter 2:   Mary's Expectation   16

Chapter 3:   The Mission of the Messiah   19

Chapter 4:   Jesus' Disciples' Expectations   28

Chapter 5:   Jesus' Expectations   34

Chapter 6:   Satan's Expectations   44

Chapter 7:   The Apostles' Expectations   51

Chapter 8:   Augustine's Expectation   60

Chapter 9:   Expectations Throughout Christian History   66

Chapter 10: Expectations of the Adventist Pioneers Before 1844 71

Chapter 11: The Aftermath of the Great Disappointment   84

Chapter 12: From Confusion to Unity   92

Chapter 13: Expectations of the Adventist Pioneers After 1850 103

Chapter 14: Adventist Expectations in the Late 1800s   108

Chapter 15: Expectations Today   118

Chapter 16: So What Lies Ahead?   127

Chapter 17: Fearful End-Time Expectations   137

Chapter 18: How to Prepare for the Final Crisis—Part 1   143

Chapter 19: How to Prepare for the Final Crisis—Part 2   153

FOREWORD:
A TRIBUTE TO MARVIN MOORE

Precious in the sight of the LORD is the death of his faithful servants.
—Psalm 116:15

In your hands, you hold the final book authored by Marvin Moore. On September 27, 2021, we here at Pacific Press® were saddened to say goodbye to our dear friend and colleague. Marvin now rests in the hope he so passionately wrote about, the glorious return of Jesus Christ. However, his voice has not been silenced; his books and articles will continue to win people to Jesus and inspire confidence in the Word of God.

Marvin served at Pacific Press® for a total of 36 years, first as a book editor and, for the last 27 years, as editor of *Signs of the Times®*. His heart for people and his zeal for the gospel powered his tireless devotion to proclaiming God's Word. With deep gratitude, we say, "Thank you, Marvin, for your faithful service. We can't wait to see you again in the earth made new."

Marvin was a prolific writer, authoring over 40 books and magazine articles too numerous to count. He was a popular speaker at churches and camp meetings. His favorite topics were the gospel of Jesus Christ and the hope-filled themes of prophecy and end-time events.

Reflecting on Marvin's life, Elder Ted N. C. Wilson, president of the General Conference of Seventh-day Adventists, said, "Marvin was a stalwart defender of God's biblical truth and as a scholar had a special gift in prodding people's thinking towards eternal truth. . . . Many people will be in heaven because of their contact with *Signs of the Times* and Marvin's work."

As you read this book and consider the tumultuous times in which we live, we sincerely desire that you will take heart from Marvin's thought-provoking words and hold fast to the promise of Jesus' soon return.

—The Publishers

INTRODUCTION

The pioneers of the Seventh-day Adventist Church would have been horrified to know that the church and the world would still be around for at least another 175 years. I'm reminded of the title of an editorial written by Loren Seibold, the editor of *Adventist Today*. It bore the clever title, "It's Too Late to Be Soon." His point was that Seventh-day Adventists have been predicting the approach of Christ's second coming for 175 years, and it still hasn't happened. Therefore, how soon is soon? It's too late to be soon!

Elizabeth Talbot, in her book *The Exodus Journey*, explains the disappointment that follows our unmet expectations: "To have high expectations and then feel your heart sinking when they are not met is very devastating. I am sure you know what I am talking about. When our expectations are shattered, it may seem unrealistic to give up anxiety and welcome trust instead. Yet God uses such situations to reveal a new aspect of His care for us."[1]

Of course, it's true that we cannot know the date of Christ's coming—or even the year, the decade, or the century—though I would like to believe that Jesus will return before the year 2100! Is that just my misguided expectation? I'll deal with that in the following chapters. For now, I can assure you of one thing: Jesus will return someday. And after almost 2,000 years since He left this earth and more than 175 years since 1844, we can be certain that His return is closer today than it was then! But can we know more? Yes and no—or no and yes. Keep reading.

---

1. Elizabeth Viera Talbot, *The Exodus Journey* (Nampa, ID: Pacific Press®, 2020), 68.

Chapter 1

ABRAHAM'S EXPECTATION

Abram was just dropping off to sleep one night when he was roused out of his slumber by a voice speaking to him. Startled, he sat up in his bed, trying not to wake Sarai up. He cocked his head, trying to hear the voice. Then it came again:

"Go from your country, your people and your father's household to the land I will show you.
"I will make you into a great nation,
  and I will bless you;
I will make your name great,
  and you will be a blessing.
I will bless those who bless you,
  and whoever curses you I will curse;
and all peoples on earth
  will be blessed through you" (Genesis 12:1–3).

Two thoughts must have struck Abram when God finished talking to him. First, he realized that this wasn't a dream. He had been wide awake, and the voice was as real as if the One speaking had been sitting in front of him. This had to be God talking to him! And second, the implication of what God had said could mean only one thing. If a nation was to arise out of his descendants, then that had to mean he was going to have a son! And this was especially good news because in all their forty or fifty years of marriage, Sarai had never gotten pregnant.

I can see Abram turning to Sarai and gently touching her, trying to wake her up. When she finally rouses and yawns, he says, "Honey, God just spoke to me, and He told me that we are going to have a son!"

Sarai is wide awake now. "What on earth!" she replies. "Honey, please don't rub it in!"

"No, dear, it's true. God just spoke to me, and He told me that He's going to make a great nation out of my descendants, and in order for that to happen, you will have to get pregnant and give birth to a son!"

The next evening Abram and Sarai are together in each other's arms. Unfortunately, a few weeks later, Sarai realizes she's not pregnant. Abram assures her that God *really did* promise that they would have a son, so they keep trying. A year goes by. Two years. Three years. Five years. Ten years (Genesis 16:3). No son! Even Abram is beginning to doubt whether God really has spoken to him!

Then one night, God appears to Abram again in a vision. "Do not be afraid, Abram," He says. "I am your shield, your very great reward" (Genesis 15:1).

We'll never know what God intended to say next because Abram interrupts Him: "Sovereign Lord," he says, "what can you give me since I remain childless" (verse 2)? In other words, "Lord, what's going on! This child You promised to give Sarai and me ten years ago still hasn't shown up!"

Please notice what's going on here. Ten years earlier, God had promised Abram that he would have a son. God didn't put a timeline on that promise. He just said, "I will make you into a great nation." And the point is this: Abram *expected* that Sarai would give birth to a son within the next year or two. But time went on and on and on, and Abram began to wonder, *When is this son going to be born?* Ten years go by, and he's beginning to have real doubts about God's promise. He's beginning to think of alternatives. In that culture, when a well-to-do family could not produce a male child to inherit the family's wealth, it was customary for the inheritance to be turned over to the family's chief male servant. And that's what Abram proposes. So Abram says, "Sovereign Lord, what can you give me since I remain childless and the one who will inherit my estate is Eliezer of Damascus?" But God says no! "A son who is your own flesh and blood will be your heir" (verses 2, 4).

So Abram tells Sarai what God had told him. But by this time, Sarai has become skeptical of Abram's so-called "encounters with God" and God's so-called "promises of a son," and she's sick and tired of hearing about it. After all, ten years earlier, when God first made the promise, there was still hope that she could conceive.[1] But now, conception is out of the question, which is why Sarai is so skeptical of the whole thing. So, she snaps back at Abram, "Husband of mine, I'm tired hearing all this nonsense about me having a son! If you're so determined to have that son you say God promised you, then take my handmaid, Hagar. Go and have a child by her!" (See Genesis 16:1, 2.) It's a spur-of-the-moment reaction that she will come to regret. However, in that culture, it was considered an acceptable way to pass down the family name to future generations.

So Abram thinks about it: *God told me that the son would come from my body. He didn't say it had to come from Sarai's body. So, OK, I'll do it!* And he sleeps with Hagar, who conceives on the first attempt! How must that have made Sarai feel?

It's easy for you and me, with knowledge of the whole story, to overlook the issue of Abram's expectation. However, it plays a critical role in what's going on. Abram doesn't know what you and I know. So, when Ishmael is born, he figures, This *is the son God promised to give me!* As Ishmael grows up, Abram tells him about God's promise and that he is the one who will fulfill that promise. God even told Hagar, "I will increase your descendants so much that they will be too numerous to count" (verse 10). And that seemed to fit perfectly with what God had told Abram ten years earlier when He said, "I will make you into a great nation" (Genesis 12:2). He's thrilled that his expectation of God's promise of a son has been fulfilled! It's what Abram told Ishmael, and that's what everyone in Abram's camp believed.

How wrong he was, as you and I know!

Fast-forward 13 years. God comes to Abram again. "I am God Almighty," He says. "Walk before me faithfully and be blameless" (Genesis 17:1). Then He changes Abram's name to Abraham.[2] It's at this point that God gives Abraham the rite of circumcision, which has been practiced by both Jews and Muslims ever since. However, what's significant for our purpose is the fact that when God repeated His promise to give Abraham a son, He said the son would be born *by Sarai*: "As for Sarai your wife, you are no longer to call her Sarai; her name will be Sarah"[3] (verse 15). And then He said, "I will bless her and will surely give you a son by her. I will bless her so that she will be the mother of nations; kings of peoples will come from her" (verse 16).

The Bible says that "Abraham fell facedown; he laughed and said to himself, 'Will a son be born to a man a hundred years old? Will Sarah bear a child at the age of ninety?' . . . 'If only Ishmael might live under your blessing!' " (verses 17, 18).

So, for 13 years, Abraham had believed that Ishmael was the son of the promise, and God went on to assure Abraham that He would indeed bless Ishmael and make him a great nation (verse 20). But He said, "My covenant I will establish with Isaac, whom Sarah will bear to you by this time next year" (verse 21; see also Genesis 18:10–12). And sure enough, miracle of all miracles, a year later, Sarah gives birth to Isaac at the ripe old age of ninety!

Abraham's expectation

One of the interesting things about God's promises is that He doesn't usually give a timeline for when they will be fulfilled, nor does He necessarily tell us what will happen between the time He gives the promise and the time it's fulfilled. This was certainly true in Abram's case. When God first came to him with the promise that he would have descendants, his immediate expectation was that Sarai would become pregnant within the next month or so. But that didn't happen, and as time went on, Abram became frustrated to the point that he began to look for alternative explanations, such as that his chief servant would be the heir. He even yielded to Sarai's suggestion that he should have a son by Hagar.

God could have intervened to stop Abram from trying to fulfill the promise his own way by having a son through Hagar, but He didn't. You and I also sometimes make mistakes when our expectations aren't fulfilled—and God doesn't intervene to prevent us from making those mistakes. But neither does He condemn us for making them. The biblical record doesn't include a single word from God reprimanding Abram for having a son by Hagar. He let him make that mistake, and He worked around it.

God also lets us live with the consequences of our mistaken expectations and the foolish things we do because of them, and Abram had to live with the consequences of his mistake of having that child by Hagar. Life became much more difficult for him and Sarai after he fathered Ishmael. Indeed, our world today is still living with the consequence of Abram's choice. The conflict between the Muslim East and the Christian West is a conflict between Christians, the descendants of Isaac, and Muslims, who are the descendants of Ishmael. These two religions are still battling it out for supremacy over the world.

Abraham's expectations are a good foretaste of the expectations that God's people have had from the time of Christ and His apostles to the present. And those expectations all have to do with the coming of the Messiah, Christ.

---

1. By the age of 65, all women today are beyond child-bearing age. See WHO Scientific Group on Research on the Menopause in the 1990s, *Research on the Menopause in the 1990s* (Geneva: World Health Organization, 1994), 14. But Sarai died when she was 127 (Genesis 23:1), so it's reasonable to assume that at age 65, she may not yet have reached menopause.

2. The name *Abram* means "exalted father," Francis D. Nichol, ed., *The Seventh-day Adventist Bible Commentary*, vol. 1 (Washington, DC: Review and Herald®, 1978), 321; *Abraham* means "father of many," *Encyclopædia Britannica Online*, s.v. "Abraham," accessed December 8, 2021, https://www.britannica.com/biography/Abraham/additional-info#history.

3. The name *Sarai* means "princess," Francis D. Nichol, ed., *The Seventh-day Adventist Bible Commentary* (Washington, DC: Review and Herald®, 1978), 1:323; *Sarah* means "woman of high rank," "Sarah," Elizabeth A. Sackler Center for Feminist Art, Brooklyn Museum, accessed December 8, 2021, https://www.brooklynmuseum.org/eascfa/dinner_party/heritage_floor/sarah.

Chapter 2

MARY'S EXPECTATION

Imagine that you are Mary, the mother of Jesus, and one day you've just arrived back home from drawing a bucket of water from the local well. You've set the bucket down, and you've bent over to clean up a scrap of food that dropped onto the floor the last time you prepared a meal when suddenly a bright light floods your kitchen. Terrified that someone has invaded your home, you whirl around, throw your hand to your mouth, and gasp: "Oh!"

On the other side of the room is a bright, shining being you've never seen before, never even imagined in your wildest dreams. You're too frightened to ask who he is, but you don't have to because he speaks first:

"Greetings, you who are highly favored! The Lord is with you" (Luke 1:28).

Your immediate reaction is, *What on earth! Who are you, and why have you come to see me?*

But the angel doesn't wait for you to ask who he is. He immediately explains his mission: "Do not be afraid, Mary; you have found favor with God. You will conceive and give birth to a son, and you are to call him Jesus. He will be great and will be called the Son of the Most High. The Lord God will give him the throne of his father David, and he will reign over Jacob's descendants forever; his kingdom will never end" (verses 30–33).

These words can mean only one thing: you will give birth to the promised Messiah—the One that God's people have looked forward to ever since the last in-person visit that Adam and Eve had with God in

Eden. At this point, you have a very serious question—a question that any young, unmarried woman would ask under the same circumstances: "How will this be," you ask, "since I am a virgin?" (verse 34).

Gabriel answers, "The Holy Spirit will come on you, and the power of the Most High will overshadow you. So the holy one to be born will be called the Son of God" (verse 35).

I wonder if Mary slept at all that night. I wonder what she told her parents and what their reaction was. We'll learn the answer to these questions when we get to heaven. But there's one other question I'd like for you to ponder: What do you suppose Mary expected to happen following the angel's visit? That she would expect to have a Child is obvious, but what did she expect that Child to accomplish when He grew up?

Well, let's look again at what Gabriel told her: "The Lord God will give him the throne of his father David, and he will reign over Jacob's descendants forever; his kingdom will never end" (verses 32, 33). Mary was no doubt familiar with Nebuchadnezzar's vision about a great image that was struck on the feet with a huge boulder that shattered the image and became a huge mountain that filled the whole earth, and she would have known that this was a prediction of the Messiah's eternal kingdom!

Mary would certainly also have known about Daniel's prediction that the Messiah would come 483 years after the command to restore and build Jerusalem (Daniel 9:25), and she would have been very aware that those 483 years were about to end. After all, the theological experts in Jerusalem would have informed the entire Jewish nation about this, and everyone was in high anticipation of the coming Messiah, who would, of course, overthrow the Romans and make the Jews the rulers of the world. *That's* what Mary would have expected her Son to accomplish during His life. *And she was to have the privilege of giving birth to that Child!*

Expectations!

In my imagination, I can see Mary in *her* imagination picturing her Son leading the armies of Israel to victory over the Romans the same way Joshua's army a millennium and a half earlier had led the armies of Israel to defeat the nations that possessed the land of Canaan. After all, the same God who gave Israel victory over the Canaanites could easily, under the leadership of her Son, give modern Israel victory over the Romans!

Great expectations!

Fast-forward thirty-four or thirty-five years. Far from her Son leading the armies of Israel to victory over the Romans, the Romans nail her Son to a cross, where six hours later He dies the cruelest of deaths. Could anything be more confusing to any human being alive at the time? Her Son is supposed to be given the throne of David and set up God's eternal kingdom; but instead, He's crucified by Israel's worst enemy! *Gabriel, where are you? What happened? Please come and explain to me what's going on!*

Expectations crushed!

Chapter 3

THE MISSION OF THE MESSIAH

S top to think for a moment of how Joseph must have felt when he got wind that his beloved Mary was pregnant. It could only mean one thing: *she had violated her commitment to marry him.* Surely she explained to him that the angel Gabriel had appeared to her and told her that she, a virgin, would give birth to the Messiah, but that was such a far-fetched excuse! I'm sure she begged and pleaded with weeping and tears. But I'm sure Joseph could scarcely believe it. We can only imagine the intense pain that both Joseph and Mary must have felt—Joseph because his beloved Mary had committed adultery and Mary because she couldn't convince him to believe her story.

In that culture, the penalty for adultery was death by stoning (Leviticus 20:10). But Joseph cared about Mary in spite of what she had "done." He didn't want to see her put to death, so he decided to "divorce her quietly" (Matthew 1:19). This would free him from the responsibility of being a father to the Child she would give birth to, and at the same time, it would spare him from having to accuse Mary of adultery.

Enter an "angel of the Lord," who came to Joseph in a dream one night shortly after Mary's encounter with Gabriel. "Joseph son of David," the angel said, "do not be afraid to take Mary home as your wife, because what is conceived in her is from the Holy Spirit" (Matthew 1:20).

So Mary *was* right! The angel Gabriel indeed *had* appeared to her that day in the kitchen; he *had* told her that she would give birth to a Son, who would be the Messiah; and the conception *was indeed* the miraculous work of the Holy Spirit in her womb!

I'm sure Joseph could hardly wait till morning to rush over to Mary's home and share with her what the angel had told *him*! It must have been a tremendous relief to Mary. And it would have been a relief to her parents, who must surely have been as skeptical of her story as Joseph had been. After all, babies don't just grow in a woman's body without some contribution from a male of the species!

The popular view of the Messiah's mission

Both of the angel's visits with Joseph and Mary have a lot to say about the mission of the Messiah, but before we get to that, let's take a look at the common Jewish understanding of the Messiah's mission in the early first century AD.

Everyone was looking forward expectantly to the Messiah's appearing. They believed that He would organize the armies of Israel and lead them to victory over the despised Roman Empire. After all, the God who had led Joshua's small, untrained army to victory over the giants who ruled Canaan 1,500 years earlier could surely, under the leadership of His powerful Messiah, lead Israel's army to victory over the hated Romans! That's exactly what every Jew at the time expected the Messiah to accomplish.

And they had a biblical basis for that conclusion. They understood Balaam's prophecy about a star rising out of Judah to refer to the Messiah's defeat of His political enemies. Here's what Balaam had said:

"I see him, but not now;
   I behold him, but not near.
A star will come out of Jacob;
   a scepter will rise out of Israel.
He will crush the foreheads of Moab,
   the skulls of all the people of Sheth.
Edom will be conquered;
   Seir, his enemy, will be conquered,
   but Israel will grow strong.

A ruler will come out of Jacob
> and destroy the survivors of the city" (Numbers 24:17–19).

This Star, this Ruler who would come out of Jacob, was clearly the Messiah, and He would conquer the nations that opposed the Jews. And, of course, in the early first century AD, the Roman Empire was Israel's worst enemy. The idea that the Messiah would conquer Rome was a foregone conclusion.

Then there's Isaiah 9:6, 7, which says:

For to us a child is born,
> to us a son is given,
> and the government will be on his shoulders.
And he will be called
> Wonderful Counselor, Mighty God,
> Everlasting Father, Prince of Peace.
Of the greatness of his government and peace
> there will be no end.
He will reign on David's throne
> and over his kingdom,
establishing and upholding it
> with justice and righteousness
> from that time on and forever.
The zeal of the LORD Almighty
> will accomplish this.

It could hardly be more obvious! The Messiah would establish the eternal kingdom that was foretold by the rock that crushed Nebuchadnezzar's great image—the stone that would "crush all those [other] kingdoms and bring them to an end, but it [God's kingdom] will itself endure forever" (Daniel 2:44).

Furthermore, the time was ripe for all this to happen. Daniel's 69-week prophecy (Daniel 7:25) pointing to the time of the Messiah's arrival was close to being fulfilled. Surely, God's eternal kingdom was about to be ushered in! And, of course, the Jewish leaders would all hold very high positions in this new world government. *That was one heady expectation!*

The Messiah's arrival to destroy the Roman Empire *had* to be near!

Joseph's dream

Gabriel's words to Mary seemed to clearly support the prevailing view. Hadn't he told her that the Child she gave birth to would "be great and will be called the Son of the Most High" (Luke 1:32)? Hadn't he said that "the Lord God will give him the throne of his father David" (verse 32)? Hadn't he assured her that her Son would "reign over Jacob's descendants forever" and "his kingdom will never end" (verse 33)?

This expectation was actually very misguided. The reason? It wasn't the Messiah's only mission. Another mission was revealed to Joseph by the angel visitor in his dream, and it had two parts. In the first part, the angel said that Mary's Child would "save his people from their sins" (Matthew 1:21). Apparently, it had never occurred to the Jewish leaders or to anyone else in that culture that before the Messiah could establish His eternal kingdom, He had to resolve the sin problem; He had to pay the death penalty for human sin. This is especially evident in Isaiah 53, which clearly is also a Messianic prophecy. Here are several of the most relevant statements:

> But he was pierced for our transgressions,
>   he was crushed for our iniquities;
> the punishment that brought us peace was on him,
>   and by his wounds we are healed (verse 5).

> For he was cut off from the land of the living;
>   for the transgression of my people he was punished.
> He was assigned a grave with the wicked,
>   and with the rich in his death,
> though he had done no violence,
>   nor was any deceit in his mouth (verses 8, 9).

For he bore the sin of many,
    and made intercession for the transgressors (verse 12).

And there was yet another part of the Messiah's mission that the angel revealed to Joseph. He said that the Messiah would fulfill Isaiah's prediction that the Messiah would be called " 'Immanuel' (which means 'God with us')" (Matthew 1:23; see Isaiah 7:14).

Ellen White said that by the time Jesus descended from heaven to our planet, "the earth was dark through misapprehension of God."[1] This means that one of the Messiah's most important missions was to reveal the truth about God—by His own example, to reveal to human beings that God is a loving Deity who wants to save them, not destroy them. When Jesus' disciple, Philip, said, "Lord, show us the Father," Jesus replied, "Don't you know me, Philip, even after I have been among you such a long time? Anyone who has seen me has seen the Father" (John 14:8, 9). Jesus was telling Philip that He, the Messiah, was "God with us," and by looking at Him and becoming acquainted with Him, people could see what God is really like.

So the angels' visits to Mary and Joseph gave three distinct missions for the same Messiah. To Mary, Gabriel stated the Messiah's mission was to establish a kingdom that would never be destroyed. And to Joseph, the angel revealed that the Messiah's two-fold mission was to represent God's true character of love to the world and to resolve the sin problem.

These angels' proclamations to Joseph and Mary weren't the only explanations of the Messiah's mission that God gave to the Jewish nation. John the Baptist also clarified the Messianic mission.

John the Baptist

God appointed John the Baptist to be the forerunner of the coming Messiah. His mission was to prepare the world for the Messiah's arrival, including revealing to the people that the main reason for Messiah's presence among them was to save His people from their sins. He made that proclamation to his disciples the day following Jesus' baptism. Seeing Jesus walking toward him, and he pointed to Him and said, "Look, the

Lamb of God, who takes away the sin of the world!" (John 1:29). The next day John again saw Jesus, and he repeated his previous statement (verses 35, 36). He may even have introduced his disciples to Jesus, and perhaps they had an initial conversation with Him.

Be that as it may, having heard what John said about Jesus, two of John's disciples followed Jesus and spent the rest of the day with Him (verses 32–39). We can only imagine the conversations that must have taken place between the three of them. I can envision the two disciples staying awake much of the night talking with Jesus and listening to what He had to say. In any case, they became convinced that Jesus was indeed the promised Messiah, and they brought Peter to Him. And He called Philip who brought Nathanael (verses 40–49).

Matthew also shed some light on John the Baptist's proclamation of the Messiah's mission. Here's how he records it: "I baptize you with water for repentance. But after me comes one who is more powerful than I, whose sandals I am not worthy to carry. He will baptize you with the Holy Spirit and fire. His winnowing fork is in his hand, and he will clear his threshing floor, gathering his wheat into the barn and burning up the chaff with unquenchable fire" (Matthew 3:11, 12).

Please note that there isn't a word in these two verses about the Messiah establishing His eternal kingdom. John's description of the Messiah's mission is wholly spiritual: repentance for sin and baptism with the Holy Spirit, and the Holy Spirit is the only power in the world who can give God's people the ability to repent of their sins and overcome them. The only battle suggested in this passage is the battle between good and evil, with the wheat—God's true believers—being gathered into His barn (His kingdom) and the wicked being banished to eternal death.

Jesus in the temple

Additionally, there's the story of Jesus and His parents visiting the temple in Jerusalem when He was twelve years old. By this time, Jesus had spent a lot of time studying the Old Testament Scriptures, which gave Him some crucial insights into the mission of the Messiah. Also, by this time, both of His parents would have shared with Him what the angels had told them about the Messiah's mission. And His visit to the temple afforded Him the opportunity to reflect on what He had learned up to that time. Ellen White says that

> for the first time the child Jesus looked upon the temple. He saw the white-robed priests performing their solemn ministry. He beheld the bleeding victim upon the altar of sacrifice. With the worshipers He bowed in prayer, while the cloud of incense ascended before God. He witnessed the impressive rites of the paschal service. Day by day He saw their meaning more clearly. Every act seemed to be bound up with His own life. New impulses were awakening within Him. Silent and absorbed, He seemed to be studying out a great problem. The mystery of His mission was opening to the Saviour.[2]

You know the rest of the story: Jesus' parents left the temple grounds to return to their home in Nazareth, thinking that Jesus was with some friends in the caravan. But come evening, they discovered to their dismay that they had left Jerusalem without Him! Immediately, they rushed back to the city and spent the next day and a half frantically searching everywhere for Him. Oh, how they must have punished themselves with guilt for not paying closer attention to His whereabouts! And oh, how they must have prayed for God to lead them to Him! And finally, God answered their prayer: they found Him in the temple, of all places, engaged in theological conversations with some Jewish religious leaders!

Here's how Luke describes it: "After three days they found him in the temple courts, sitting among the teachers, listening to them and asking them questions. Everyone who heard him was amazed at his understanding and his answers" (Luke 2:46, 47).

Now let me ask you, what do you think Jesus was discussing with these religious leaders and teachers of the law? Ellen White tells us this: "The rabbis spoke of the wonderful elevation which the Messiah's coming would bring to the Jewish nation; but Jesus presented the prophecy of Isaiah [53], and asked them the meaning of those scriptures that point to the suffering and death of the Lamb of God.[3]

Conclusion

I have a reason for sharing with you what the angels told Mary and Joseph about the Messiah's mission, what John the Baptist said about Jesus' mission, and what Jesus in the temple shared with the religious leaders about His mission. The Jews had a very distorted understanding of the Messiah's mission. They envisioned Him coming as a conqueror of the Roman Empire, as a deliverer of the Israelites from Rome's power, a leader who would establish them as the rulers of the world. *They* would become the stone cut out from a mountain without human hands that would destroy all earthly kingdoms. *They* would be leaders in this earthly kingdom that would last forever and ever (see Daniel 2:33–35, 44, 45). Joseph, John the Baptist, and Jesus Himself revealed a much different vision of the Messiah's purpose in coming to the world. This is not to say that there will be no coming Messianic kingdom that will overthrow all earthly kingdoms.

But before the Messiah could establish His eternal kingdom on earth, He first had to resolve the conflict between good and evil by paying the death penalty for human sin. He had to reveal the truth about God that had become so distorted in human minds—even in the minds of His own people! And *that* was the purpose of His coming to earth in the first-century AD.

Jesus' entire life on this earth—everything He taught and all the miracles He wrought—was a revelation of His purpose in coming to our broken, sinful world. But His own people were so fixated on their *expectation* of the Messiah's *glorious* mission that they absolutely *could not* accept the truth about His *humble* mission in coming to the world in their day. That's why, when He came to fulfill His humble mission, they rejected Him. And because of this, when He really does come on His glorious mission to establish His eternal kingdom on the earth, they will see Him coming in the clouds of heaven, and they will call for the rocks and the mountains to fall on them and hide them "from the face of him who sits on the throne and from the wrath of the Lamb! For the great day of their wrath has come, and who can withstand it?" (Revelation 6:16, 17).

In all of this, there are extremely important lessons for us today. First, it's critical that we have correct expectations about God's plans for the future of our world and of our own personal part in it, because if we misunderstand; if we contrive false expectations, it can cost us our eternal life, just as it cost the Jewish leaders theirs! And second, expectations and mission are inextricably intertwined, which we will clearly see as we proceed through the rest of this book, for false expectations can lead to a misunderstanding of God's mission for us in the world.

---

1. Ellen G. White, *The Desire of Ages* (Mountian View, CA: Pacific Press®, 1940), 22.
2. White, 78.
3. White, 78.

Chapter 4

JESUS' DISCIPLES' EXPECTATIONS

The time had come for Jesus to explain more fully to His disciples His mission to "save his people from their sins" (Matthew 1:21) and to correct their profound expectation that the Messiah was about to establish His eternal kingdom. Jesus also knew that the crowds that surrounded Him day after day would make it difficult to engage them in a thoughtful conversation about His real mission, so He took His disciples to an isolated place in Gentile territory about twenty-five miles north of the Sea of Galilee called Caesarea Philippi[1] where they could be alone (Matthew 16:13). However, He didn't begin by telling them about the nature of His coming kingdom. He began with a question: He asked them, "Who do people say the Son of Man is?" (verse 13). Notice that He didn't begin with, Who do *you* think I am? He asked them, Who do *other people* think I am? They responded, "Some say John the Baptist; others say Elijah; and still others, Jeremiah or one of the prophets" (verse 14). Only then did Jesus ask, "Who do *you* say I am" (verse 15 emphasis added).

"Simon Peter answered, 'You are the Messiah, the Son of the living God' " (verse 16).

That was the answer Jesus was looking for! He replied, "Blessed are you, Simon son of Jonah, for this was not revealed to you by flesh and blood, but by my Father in heaven." However, He "ordered his disciples not to tell anyone that He was the Messiah" (verses 17, 20). And with this, Jesus was ready to discuss with His disciples the truth about His mission. He was ready to begin changing their expectations about His mission. "From that time on Jesus began to explain to his disciples that he must go to Jerusalem and suffer many things at the hands of the elders, the chief priests and the teachers of the law, and that he must be killed and on the third day be raised to life" (verse 21).

Unfortunately, these poor disciples were so immersed in their expectation of a Messiah whose mission was to defeat the Romans, establish an earthly kingdom, and rule on David's throne that they totally rejected the idea that He would be handed over to the Jewish rulers, who would condemn Him to death by crucifixion. And the idea that He would be raised back to life on the third day was simply absurd.

Peter rebukes Jesus

To you and me 2,000 years later, this seems as plain as day. We have the entire New Testament that explains why Jesus had to die and be resurrected. But it was obviously impossible for Jesus' disciples to know all the history that we know because it hadn't happened yet. It seemed incredible to them that the Messiah would have to die, to say nothing of being raised back to life on the third day. It was so incredible that "Peter took [Jesus] aside and began to rebuke him. 'Never, Lord!' he said. 'This shall never happen to you!' "(Matthew 16:22). Dear Peter. He was prepared to protect his Master, even if it meant his own death! In fact, that's precisely what he avowed a few months later at the time of the Last Supper in the upper room (John 13:37).

But back to Peter's affirmation that he would not allow Jesus to be crucified. Notice what Jesus did *not* say. He didn't say, "Peter, I realize that you can't understand it now, but it's really true. I will be crucified, and I will rise again the third day." No. "Jesus turned and said to Peter, 'Get behind me, Satan! You are a stumbling block to me; you do not have in mind the concerns of God, but merely human concerns' " (Matthew 16:23).

At first glance, it might seem that Jesus was overreacting extremely to Peter's misunderstanding of His mission. But Jesus knew what lay ahead for Him in the next few months: two horrible trials before the Jewish Sanhedrin and the Roman governor Pilate and a third trial before

Herod, all of which would end with the cruel torture of two whippings that would tear His back into shreds, and this would be followed by the agony of the cruel cross. *This was not a pleasant thought to Jesus.* Even at this point, several months prior to His actual crucifixion, the knowledge of what lay ahead of Him was very difficult for Him to contemplate. If I'd been in His shoes, I wouldn't have been able to sleep at night! Fortunately, if I have to die a martyr's death someday, I at least don't know about it now. But Jesus *did* know what lay ahead for Him! And you and I can only imagine how painful it would be to know that!

Satan, of course, also understood very well the mental and emotional distress Jesus would experience in Gethsemane and in the following eighteen hours. He was also keenly aware that the conflict between good and evil was nearing the climax of its first stage,* which would decide its ultimate resolution. He was determined in one way or another to defeat Christ, and he attempted to use Peter's misguided sense of Christ's mission to discourage Him from going through with it in light of the coming conflict.

This account illustrates the importance of having accurate biblical expectations about the future. Peter's misunderstanding of the Messiah's mission in his day led directly to him becoming a tool of Satan. It led him to inadvertently tempt Jesus to give up His mission to save His people from their sins! And I propose that the same is true for us today. If we have incorrect expectations about the coming crisis and Christ's second coming, we, too, can easily succumb to Satan's deceptions that will not only threaten our own eternal life but also cause others to lose theirs. And if we have false expectations about the coming final crisis, it can horribly distort our understanding of the mission that God has for us both now and during that crisis.

Who will be the greatest?
The fact that Jesus' disciples totally misunderstood His mission is also evident in the ongoing debate among them as to which of them would

---

* The second stage being the world's final crisis leading up to Christ's second coming.

be the greatest in His coming kingdom (Mark 9:33, 34). They kept vying among themselves as to which one would hold the highest and most honorable positions. The mother of James and John even had the audacity to ask Jesus to give her sons the two highest positions in that kingdom—an act that aroused a huge feeling of jealousy among the other ten disciples, who resented her barging into what was none of her business. Jesus had to call them together and explain to them that the one who would be the greatest in His kingdom would be the one who was their most humble servant (Matthew 20:24–28). Unfortunately, they still didn't get it. As late as their final meal with their Master, they were still debating among themselves as to which one would be the greatest in the kingdom. Ellen White's chapter "A Servant of Servants" in *The Desire of Ages* is about Jesus washing His disciples' feet at the last supper, and she points out the contention and jealousy that filled the minds of His disciples as they entered the upper room:

> The disciples clung to their favorite idea that Christ would assert His power, and take His position on the throne of David. And in heart each still longed for the highest place in the kingdom. They had placed their own estimate upon themselves and upon one another, and, instead of regarding their brethren as more worthy, they had placed themselves first. The request of James and John to sit on the right and left of Christ's throne had excited the indignation of the others. That the two brothers should presume to ask for the highest position so stirred the ten that alienation threatened. They felt that they were misjudged, that their fidelity and talents were not appreciated. Judas was the most severe upon James and John.
>
> When the disciples entered the supper room, their hearts were full of resentful feelings. Judas pressed next to Christ on the left side; John was on the right. If there was a highest place, Judas was determined to have it, and that place was thought to be next to Christ. And Judas was a traitor.[2]

Judas's betrayal of Jesus

This misunderstanding of Christ's mission led directly to Judas's decision to betray Him. To quote Ellen White again, "Judas was continually advancing the idea that Christ would reign as king in Jerusalem."[3] "The prospect of having a high place in the new kingdom had led Judas to espouse the cause of Christ. Were his hopes [his expectations] to be disappointed?"[4] In fact, they *were* disappointed—but not until after he had betrayed Jesus. He thought that in betraying Him to the Jewish leaders, he would force Him to declare Himself to be the Messiah and establish His earthly kingdom, and *he, Judas,* "would have the credit of having placed the king on David's throne. And this act would secure to him the first position, next to Christ, in the new kingdom."[5] That is the length to which false expectations can lead people when they are religious in name only and not in heart!

And while the rest of Jesus' disciples remained loyal to Him during His trial and crucifixion, their anguish over His crucifixion was not just pity for the torture He endured. Their excruciating pain was especially prompted by the great disappointment that their hopes of Jesus establishing His earthly kingdom had been crushed. "At the very time when they expected to see their Lord ascend the throne of David, they beheld Him seized as a malefactor, scourged, derided, and condemned, and lifted up on the cross of Calvary."[6] As the disciples who walked with Him on the road to Emmaus said during their conversation, "We had hoped that he was the one who was going to redeem Israel" (Luke 24:21). Of course, that's exactly what Jesus *did* accomplish. By His death on the cross, He redeemed not just Israel but the entire world from sin's death penalty. But His disciples failed to understand this. It took His dramatic death on the cross to disabuse all of His disciples of their false expectations about His mission.

Now that He had died and risen again, He could explain His real mission to them, and they would be more ready to understand. As Luke tells the story, Jesus said to these two disciples: " 'How foolish you are, and how slow to believe *all* that the prophets have spoken! Did not the Messiah have to suffer these things and then enter his glory?'

And beginning with Moses and all the Prophets, he explained to them what was said in *all* the Scriptures concerning himself" (verses 25–27, emphasis added).

Yet they still didn't totally "get it." Yes, they now understood that Jesus had to die to redeem at least the Jews from their sins, but just before Jesus ascended to heaven, His disciples again asked Him, "Are you at this time going to restore the kingdom to Israel?" (Acts 1:6). False expectations do die hard! And it took several more years for Jesus' Jewish disciples to realize that He also died to save the Gentiles (see Acts 10; 15). And even then, there was pressure from conservative Jewish Christians to think they were better than the Gentiles (see Galatians 2:11–14).

Allow me to suggest an important lesson that we can learn from this chapter: mission and expectations are so closely linked that if we get one wrong, we will almost certainly get the other one wrong. Also mission influences expectations, not the other way around. If you have a correct understanding of your mission, you're much more likely to have a reasonable expectation of how that mission will end. We will see the outworking of this principle several times in the remainder of this book.

1. See F. D. Nichol, ed., *The Seventh-day Adventist Bible Commentary* (Washington, DC: Review and Herald®, 1956), 5:428.

2. Ellen G. White, *The Desire of Ages* (Mountian View, CA: Pacific Press®, 1940), 643, 644.

3. White, 718.

4. White, 718.

5. White, 721.

6. Ellen G. White, *The Great Controversy* (Mountain View, CA: Pacific Press®, 1950), 345, 346.

Chapter 5

JESUS' EXPECTATIONS

J esus is our model. We need to pattern our lives after His. And that includes His understanding of His mission, His expectations that arose out of His mission, and how He dealt with both. Then we need to follow His example as we deal with our own mission and the expectations that arise out of that mission. I will begin by pointing out that during His adult years, Jesus had a very accurate understanding of His mission and the suffering He could expect to result from it. I will explain what I mean as we go through this chapter.

Jesus had no idea of His mission when He was first born, nor did He most likely understand anything about it for the first few years of His life. Mary and Joseph understood something about it, as I pointed out in an earlier chapter, and I'm sure that, starting perhaps when He was five or six years old, they told Him the three things they knew: (1) that He was the promised Messiah, (2) that He would save His people from their sins, and (3) that someday He would reign on David's throne. They no doubt introduced these ideas to Him gradually, as they felt He was able to understand them. And the Holy Spirit would surely have guided them through this process.

Of course, *their* understanding of the Messiah's mission would have been influenced by the Jewish culture in which they grew up, and their explanations would have reflected these ideas. I'm sure Jesus also attended the local synagogue every Sabbath and perhaps at other times during the week, so between that and His own parents' understanding of the Messiah's mission, He became thoroughly acquainted with the popular view that the

Messiah would establish an earthly kingdom and conquer the Romans.

So, given this popular expectation, how did Jesus come to a correct understanding of His mission? My guess is that it came to Him gradually. One thing we do know is that He did not attend the schools of the rabbis, where He would have been indoctrinated into the popular view. Ellen White said, "The child Jesus did not receive instruction in the synagogue schools. His mother was His first human teacher. From her lips and from the scrolls of the prophets, He learned of heavenly things."[1]

I've sometimes wondered how Jesus gained access to these scrolls. Most Christians today have several Bibles in their possession—but not Jesus! In His day, the Old Testament scrolls were few and far between and *very* expensive. Most of them were kept in the synagogues for use during the Sabbath services. Jesus' parents were very poor, and I can't imagine that they had a large collection of them—or even one! So did Jesus get the permission of the ruler of the synagogue in Nazareth to read them? It's a question I'll be interested in learning the answer to when I get to heaven. However, He gained access to the scrolls. As He got older, Jesus must have spent a lot of time studying and memorizing them. Ellen White said that "His intimate acquaintance with the Scriptures shows how diligently His early years were given to the study of God's word."[2]

During His careful study and reflection, He would surely have noticed the two views of the Messiah's mission. On the one hand, the angel told Mary that her Son would be "great and will be called the Son of the Most High. The Lord God will give him the throne of his father David, and he will reign over Jacob's descendants forever" (Luke 1:32, 33). And this agreed with the words of Isaiah. He said that the Messiah would be called

> Mighty God,
> Everlasting Father, Prince of Peace.
> Of the greatness of His government and peace
>   there will be no end.
> He will reign on David's throne
>   and over his kingdom,
> establishing and upholding it

with justice and righteousness
from that time on and forever (Isaiah 9:6, 7).

On the other hand, an angel told Joseph that Mary's Son would "save
his people from their sins" (Matthew 1:21), also agreeing with Isaiah
who said that the Messiah would "[take] up our pain and [bear] our
suffering" (Isaiah 53:4). He would be "pierced for our transgressions"
and "crushed for our iniquities" (verse 5). He would be "numbered with
the transgressors," and He would "[bear] the sin of many" (verse 12).

How could it be both ways? How could Jesus be the King who sits
on David's throne forever and at the same time suffer and die to save
His people from their sins? These, I suspect, are some of the questions
that Jesus had to wrestle with during His growing-up years. Fortunately,
Jesus had the Holy Spirit guiding His thoughts. After all, Jesus told His
and disciples that the Holy Spirit would "guide [them] into all the truth"
(John 16:13), and surely the same Holy Spirit guided Jesus as He tried
to understand the truth about His mission to the world!

Jesus visits the temple

I've already pointed out to you that at some point, probably no later
than when He was five or six years old, Jesus' parents began explaining
His mission to Him. At first, they may have simply told Him that God
had great plans for His life. But as He grew older, they would have told
Him that He was the Messiah, and they would have shared with Him
what the angels had told them about His mission. This, combined with
His own study of the Scriptures, would have gotten Jesus started in
understanding His mission. A very significant event that helped Jesus
to understand His mission more clearly was His visit with His parents
to the temple in Jerusalem when He was twelve years old.

Let's take another look at what Ellen White wrote describing that
event:

For the first time the child Jesus looked upon the temple. He saw
the white-robed priests performing their solemn ministry. He

beheld the bleeding victim upon the altar of sacrifice. With the worshipers He bowed in prayer, while the cloud of incense ascended before God. He witnessed the impressive rites of the paschal service. *Day by day He saw their meaning more clearly. Every act seemed to be bound up with His own life.* New impulses were awakening within Him. Silent and absorbed, He seemed to be studying out a great problem. *The mystery of His mission was opening to the Saviour.*[3]

Consider these points carefully:
- Day by day He saw the meaning of the sacrifices more clearly.
- Every act of the paschal service seemed bound up with His own life.
- "Silent and absorbed, He seemed to be studying out a great problem."
- The mystery of His mission was opening to Him.

I can't help but wonder what it would be like to be a 12-year-old child who realizes that in some way, somehow, He was going to have to die to pay for the sins of the world! One must also conclude that what Jesus learned from the sacrificial system during His visit to the temple contributed to the questions He asked the teachers of the law toward the end of His stay in Jerusalem.

The wilderness temptation
Fast-forward another eighteen years. Jesus' Father speaks to Him from the heavens following His baptism, saying, "This is my Son, whom I love; with him I am well pleased" (Matthew 3:17). This is the first time the Bible records Jesus receiving communication from God, though I can't help but suspect that He may have had revelations and perhaps even direct communication with God and/or angels during His growing up years in Nazareth.

Be that as it may, a little more than a month after His baptism, Jesus was confronted by Satan following His 40-day fast in the wilderness. And by this time, Jesus knew for certain what lay ahead for Him during His stay on earth. Put another way; He had a very accurate *expectation* regarding His fate near the end of His earthly mission. He knew that He would be tried, condemned, and executed by crucifixion. He also knew that He would be resurrected the third day after His death and that shortly after that, He would return to heaven to carry out His mediatorial ministry for those who believed in Him. But Satan was desperate to get Jesus to give up His mission to pay the price for human sin, so he offered Him the kingdom on much easier terms: "Jesus, you don't have to go through all that pain and torture a few years from now. Just bow down and worship me, and the whole world will be Yours."

Jesus, knowing just what to expect three-and-a-half years later, turned down Satan's offer! Imagine what would have happened had Jesus misunderstood His mission and had had a distorted expectation of His future. His expectation went beyond the trial, the torture, and the crucifixion He would experience. His expectation extended to His victory over Satan by His resurrection from the dead. It's because of this very accurate expectation that He was able to defeat Satan in the wilderness.

Peter tempts Jesus
A couple of years later, with only a year or so left on earth, Jesus decided that it was time to begin revealing to His disciples the trauma He and they would endure at His trial and crucifixion. He also wanted to share the good news that three days afterward, He would rise from the dead. Unfortunately, as I pointed out in a previous chapter, the disciples were so immersed in their own expectation that Jesus would establish His political kingdom on earth that they simply could not get it through their heads that their precious Messiah would be crucified! This was unthinkable—ridiculous! Jesus' expectation about His future came to a traumatic collision with their expectation about His future. The conversation escalated to the point that Peter said, "Jesus, come with me." He took Him off to one side and said, "Never, Lord! . . . This shall never happen to you!" (Matthew 16:22).

Jesus didn't argue with Peter. It was at this point that He said *very firmly*, "Get behind me, Satan! You are a stumbling block to me; you do not have in mind the concerns of God, but merely human concerns" (Matthew 16:23).

I'd be very interested in knowing Peter's reaction; but Matthew doesn't say anything about that. But he must have been shocked. "Jesus, You're calling me Satan? How can you do that!" Maybe someday in heaven, you and I can read God's record of that conversation and learn how Peter responded. But for now, we don't need to know.

The point is that Jesus knew just what He was going to face a few months later. He had a very accurate expectation of what lay ahead for Him, and it wasn't pleasant to contemplate. Jesus was a human Being, after all, with a brain and nerves throughout His body just as you and I have, and the intense suffering He would have to endure wasn't any more pleasant for Him to contemplate than it would be for you and me. And Jesus understood that Satan was using His well-meaning disciple to get Him to abandon His mission.

Gethsemane

We come now to Jesus' final hours. At the Last Supper, He tried to warn His disciples of what lay ahead for both Him and them; but they couldn't bear the thought. He told Peter that he would deny Him, but Peter insisted on his loyalty to his Master (Mark 14:27–31; Luke 22:31–34).

I frankly have a hard time understanding how Jesus could maintain His composure in the upper room, knowing as He did what would happen to Him over the next eighteen hours. However, on the walk with His disciples to Gethsemane, Jesus began to lose that composure. Here's how Ellen White describes it:

> As they approached the garden, the disciples had marked the change that came over their Master. Never before had they seen Him so utterly sad and silent. As He proceeded, this strange sadness deepened; yet they dared not question Him as to the cause. His form swayed as if He were about to fall. Upon reaching the garden, the disciples looked anxiously for His usual place of retirement, that

their Master might rest. Every step that He now took was with labored effort. He groaned aloud, as if suffering under the pressure of a terrible burden. Twice His companions supported Him, or He would have fallen to the earth.[4]

Arriving in Gethsemane, Jesus' expectation about what was about to happen filled Him with profound anxiety, and Satan, desperate to win the conflict in the great controversy, used this opportunity to press strong doubt into Jesus' mind. Ellen White continues:

Now the tempter had come for the last fearful struggle. For this he had been preparing during the three years of Christ's ministry. Everything was at stake with him. If he failed here, his hope of mastery was lost; the kingdoms of the world would finally become Christ's; he himself would be overthrown and cast out. But if Christ could be overcome, the earth would become Satan's kingdom, and the human race would be forever in his power. With the issues of the conflict before Him, Christ's soul was filled with dread of separation from God. Satan told Him that if He became the surety for a sinful world, the separation would be eternal. He would be identified with Satan's kingdom, and would nevermore be one with God. . . .

. . . In its hardest features Satan pressed the situation upon the Redeemer.[5]

Three times, Jesus pled with His Father, "If it is possible, may this cup be taken from me. Yet not as I will, but as you will" (Matthew 26:39). His anxiety over the torture He knew He was about to experience was so severe that "his sweat was like drops of blood falling to the ground" (Luke 22:44). This is actually a phenomenon that has been seen to occur in other people during situations of intense anxiety. A forensic pathologist by the name of Frederick Zugbe, MD, PhD has noted that "there is a rare condition called hematidrosis that may occur in cases of extreme anxiety. . . . It manifests itself as sweat that contains blood or blood pigments."[6]

And what was the cause of this intense anxiety? It was Jesus' knowledge of what was about to happen to Him. Please note that I used the word *knowledge* in that sentence. I could also have said that it was Jesus' *expectation* that caused sweat mixed with blood to break out on His brow.

Now here's a critical point that I do not want you to miss: Jesus' *expectation* was absolutely correct. He wasn't born with this expectation built into His mind. He developed it gradually, through careful, Spirit-directed Bible study during His years in Nazareth and afterward. His visit to the temple in Jerusalem at the age of twelve was a major influence in His growing understanding of the mission for which God had brought Him into the world. By the time Satan tempted Him in the wilderness, He had a very clear expectation about the trial and crucifixion He would experience a few years later. That's why He told Satan, very forcefully, to "get thee behind me" (Luke 4:8, KJV)!

Partway through Jesus' prayer in Gethsemane, "an angel from heaven appeared to him and strengthened him" (Luke 22:43). Commenting on this, Ellen White writes:

In this awful crisis, when everything was at stake, when the mysterious cup trembled in the hand of the sufferer, the heavens opened, a light shone forth amid the stormy darkness of the crisis hour, and the mighty angel who stands in God's presence, occupying the position from which Satan fell, came to the side of Christ. The angel came not to take the cup from Christ's hand, but to strengthen Him to drink it, with the assurance of the Father's love. He came to give power to the divine-human suppliant. He pointed Him to the open heavens, telling Him of the souls that would be saved as the result of His sufferings. He assured Him that His Father is greater and more powerful than Satan, that His death would result in the utter discomfiture of Satan, and that the kingdom of this world would be given to the saints of the Most High. He told Him that He would see of the travail of His soul, and be satisfied, for He would see a multitude of the human race saved, eternally saved.[7]

It was enough. The angel's visit strengthened Jesus to face the crisis that lay immediately ahead of Him. Ellen White continues:

> Christ's agony did not cease, but His depression and discouragement left Him. The storm had in nowise abated, but He who was its object was strengthened to meet its fury. He came forth calm and serene. A heavenly peace rested upon His bloodstained face.[8]

All this was a part of Jesus' expectation. And now it was time for Him to enter upon that expected final trial of His life that would determine not only the fate of the human race but also provide the legal basis for the resolution of the universal conflict between good and evil. During His sham trial, Jesus endured false accusations, a crown of thorns, and two whippings of thirty-nine and forty lashes across His back. His suffering would have been so intense, especially with the whippings, that it's a wonder He survived to be crucified! And then there was the cross upon which He agonized for six hours before He finally breathed His last and exclaimed, "It is finished" (John 19:30). Then He bowed His head and said, "Father, into your hands I commit my spirit" (Luke 23:46). Praise God that Jesus understood His mission and accepted the expectation of suffering that it entailed!

In concluding this chapter, I want to point out one critical detail: In all that mob of people who followed Jesus through His trial and crucifixion, not one person understood what was really going on. Even His own mother, His disciples, and other followers had expected Him to take the throne of David and lead the armies of Israel to victory over the Roman Empire. Nobody had expected Him to die a criminal's death.

This point is so significant that I will repeat it so you won't miss it later in this book: *In all that mob of people who followed Jesus through His trial and crucifixion, not one other person understood what was really going on.* The battle that would decide Satan's fate and the fate of the world and even of the entire universe was taking place before their very eyes. The mob, influenced by the religious leaders who were inspired by Satan, thought they were just getting rid of a pesky rabbi who was getting in the way of their ambitions. And those closest to Jesus were shocked and heartbroken. They had expected an entirely different outcome.

What if Jesus had misunderstood His mission? What if *He* had not understood what was really going on? The world would not have the expectation of salvation through His death and resurrection.

That's the importance of having accurate expectations!

———————

1. Ellen G. White, *The Desire of Ages* (Mountain View, CA: Pacific Press®, 1940), 70.

2. White, 70.

3. White, 78; emphasis added.

4. White, 685, 686.

5. White, 686, 687.

6. Terry McDermott, "The Physical Effects of the Scourging and Crucifixion of Jesus," *Catholic Insight*, March 13, 2020, http://catholicinsight.com/the-physical-effects-of-the-scourging-and-crucifixion-of-Jesus.

7. White, *Desire of Ages*, 693, 694.

8. White, 694.

Chapter 6

SATAN'S EXPECTATIONS

Y ou may wonder why I have devoted an entire chapter in this book to Satan's expectations. Who cares what Satan expects? It's actually extremely important to understand Satan's expectations, for not to understand them is to risk being deceived by him. One of his most clever strategies is to understand very clearly what the future holds and then deceive you and me into *mis*understanding the future so that we won't be prepared for it.

Satan's story began in heaven thousands of years ago. He was known as Lucifer at the time. He was a very gorgeous, highly honored angel who stood in the very presence of God as His covering cherub (Ezekiel 28:12–15). But Lucifer became jealous of the fact that Michael held a higher position within the Godhead than he did, and he began whispering insinuations among some of his closest angel friends. In time, he gained sympathy from some of them, and he began to think, *Maybe I can take Michael's place in the Godhead!* He shared these thoughts with his angel friends, and as more and more of them agreed with him, he grew bold and actually challenged Michael's role openly. Finally, when fully one-third of heaven's angels sided with him (Revelation 12:3, 4, 7), Lucifer went to war to get his "rightful place" in the counsels of the Deity.

My guess is that Lucifer had fully convinced himself that he could win the conflict. This was the first of many of his expectations, and it failed. He and his loyal supporters were "not strong enough, and they lost their place in heaven. The great dragon was hurled down—that ancient serpent called the devil, or Satan, who leads the whole world astray. He was hurled to the earth, and his angels with him" (verses 8, 9).

Once he was on the earth, Satan's strategy changed completely. Instead of trying to defeat Michael and His angels, he set out to conquer Adam and Eve. God had told Adam, "You are free to eat from any tree in the garden; but you must not eat from the tree of the knowledge of good and evil, for when you eat from it you will certainly die" (Genesis 2:16, 17). I can assure you that Satan was standing nearby, and he heard what God told Adam. And Satan said to himself, *Aha! That's where I'll get them!* And from that point on, Satan began plotting to get Adam and Eve to eat the fruit from the forbidden tree.

I wouldn't say that at this point, Satan *expected* to get Adam and Eve to sin. Before they actually yielded to his temptation, the most he could do was *hope* they would yield. There's a difference between hope and expectation. *Hope* says, "This is what I would *like* to happen, what I believe *can* happen, but I can't be sure it *will* happen." On the other hand, *expectation* says, "This is what I believe *will* happen, I am quite certain that it *will* happen."

We don't know how long it took Satan to lay his plans, but my guess is that it was quite a while. He would have had to observe the two humans closely to decide which one would be the most likely to yield to his temptation, and then he would have had to devise a plan. As you know, he chose Eve. And since he could only approach her openly at the tree of the knowledge of good and evil, he would have had to wait for her to walk up to the tree alone. Finally, the day arrived, and, as we all know, Satan succeeded brilliantly!

So now, what was Satan's plan? Ellen White provided a remarkable insight into Satan's expectation after he conquered Adam and Eve:

> With intense interest the unfallen worlds had watched to see Jehovah arise, and sweep away the inhabitants of the earth. And if God should do this, Satan was ready to carry out his plan for securing to himself the allegiance of heavenly beings. He had declared that the principles of God's government make forgiveness impossible. Had the world been destroyed, he would have claimed that his

accusations were proved true. He was ready to cast blame upon God, and to spread his rebellion to the worlds above. But instead of destroying the world, God sent His Son to save it.[1]

So Satan's expectation to spread rebellion throughout the universe was shattered. However, he also learned something: when God met with Adam and Eve the day of their fall, He promised that He would send a Redeemer who would crush Satan's head (Genesis 3:15); that is, defeat him. So now it became Satan's determined effort to defeat this Redeemer when He arrived. And for the next 4,000 years, he read every scrap of divine inspiration that he could get his hands on in order to understand the prophecies about this Redeemer. To quote Ellen White again, she says that Satan "is a diligent student of the Bible, and is much better acquainted with the prophecies than many religious teachers. He knows that it is for his interest to keep well informed in the revealed purposes of God, that he may defeat the plans of the Infinite."[2]

And defeat them he did—almost. He's very good at deceiving human beings and getting them to do his bidding. He did it with Adam and Eve, and he's done it with sinful human beings ever since. Fortunately, he hasn't succeeded with every human being throughout history. He failed with Enoch and Noah; he failed with Abraham, Isaac, Jacob, and Moses. He failed with Joshua, Samuel, and David; he failed with Elijah, Elisha, Jeremiah, and Daniel; He failed with Peter, John, and Paul; and, most important, he failed with Jesus! But oh, did he ever try with Jesus! It began with Herod's attack on Jesus in His infancy; but he failed. The Bible tells us very little about Jesus' early life; however, we can be sure that Satan tried to trip Jesus up during those years, but he failed.

The first recorded incident of Satan's effort to defeat Jesus in a personal confrontation is the temptation in the wilderness. He began by pretending to be an angel from heaven who had come to "help" Jesus in His starved condition; but Jesus recognized the deception when Satan said, "*If* you are the Son of God . . ." So recognizing that Jesus was trusting God to supply His need for food, Satan tried to get Him to trust God in a flawed manner. That was the whole point of his temptation on top of the temple. But he failed. Finally, recognizing that Jesus knew exactly who He was, he used Jesus' normal human apprehension about His future trial and crucifixion to get Him to give up. He said, in effect, "Look, Jesus, I know what You're supposed to endure a few years from now, but I have a much easier way for You to achieve Your purpose of regaining the kingdom from me. Just bow down and worship me, and I will hand it over to You. It will all be Yours!

But Jesus recognized that Satan's offer of the kingdom would have actually made Him subservient to Satan, so, He said, "No!" And He kept heading toward the trial at the end of His earthly life, which was the *real* way for Him to conquer Satan and take back His kingdom.

Unfortunately, Satan was much more successful with the Jewish nation. First, he got them to believe that *they alone* were God's holy people, and *they* were better than the despicable Gentiles. From there, he led them to overlook the prophecies about a suffering Messiah and instead to gloat over all the prophecies about the coming Messianic kingdom. Jesus told them parable after parable about the *spiritual* nature of the Messianic kingdom that had to *precede* the universal one, but they would have none of it. The kingdom of glory it would be! Their beloved Messiah would lead them to defeat the Romans and establish God's political kingdom in which they, the Jewish leaders, would hold *very* prominent positions! Oh, the glory! And hadn't Daniel predicted the approximate time for the Messiah's appearing? And hadn't that time almost come?

That's what the Jewish people, especially their leaders, believed. That was their cherished expectation. But it was all a marvelous deception of Satan! And his expectations were fully met with the Jewish leadership.

But that was only part of his strategy. The most important part of Satan's strategy to defeat Jesus was to prevent Him from dying to save His people from their sins. He simply could *not* allow that to happen. For if Jesus did die as the sinless Substitute and Surety for sinful humanity, Satan would lose the universal conflict between himself and Jesus. He had lost at the temptation in the wilderness, and as Jesus began His final journey to Jerusalem, Satan was determined to defeat Him at His trial and crucifixion. After all, during those hours, Jesus would be denied His Father's presence. Here is where the Father would depart from Him so that He could die the death of the wicked. Here is where Jesus would be the most vulnerable.

The final struggle between Christ and Satan began in Gethsemane. Ellen White describes Satan's strategy.

> Satan told [Jesus] that if He became the surety for a sinful world, the separation would be eternal. He would be identified with Satan's kingdom, and would nevermore be one with God. . . .
>
> . . . In its hardest features Satan pressed the situation upon the Redeemer: The people who claim to be above all others in temporal and spiritual advantages have rejected You. They are seeking to destroy You, the foundation, the center and seal of the promises made to them as a peculiar people. One of Your own disciples, who has listened to Your instruction, and has been among the foremost in church activities, will betray You. One of Your most zealous followers will deny You. All will forsake You. Christ's whole being abhorred the thought. That those whom He had undertaken to save, those whom He loved so much, should unite in the plots of Satan, this pierced His soul. The conflict was terrible.[3]

But to Satan's horror, Jesus endured Gethsemane and allowed Himself to be arrested. Next came the trial, and here Satan pulled out all the stops. The mental and physical pain Satan instigated in the hearing before the Sanhedrin, where Jesus was slapped and ridiculed, was bad enough. But then came the trial before Pilate, and the whippings, where the pain was so severe that many criminals who experienced it died even before the whipping was over. And finally, there was the cross, where the pain from the nails being driven through His hands caused the Savior intense anguish. And when the cross was dropped into the hole, He would have, once again, experienced severe agony. The six hours He hung on the cross were sheer torture.* But finally, it was over. Jesus cried out, "Father, into your hands I commit my spirit" (Luke 23:46), and He hung His head and died.

And Satan lost.

Ah, but there was still one more chance that he might win—if he could just hold Jesus in the tomb! Ellen White described the scene: "When Jesus was laid in the grave, Satan triumphed. He dared to hope [expect] that the Saviour would not take up His life again. He claimed the Lord's body, and set his guard about the tomb, seeking to hold Christ a prisoner."[4]

Then, as dawn approached

the great stone was in its place; the Roman seal was unbroken; the Roman guards were keeping their watch. And there were unseen watchers. Hosts of evil angels were gathered about the place. Had it been possible, the prince of darkness with his apostate army would have kept forever sealed the tomb that held the Son of God. But a heavenly host surrounded the sepulcher. Angels that excel in strength were guarding the tomb, and waiting to welcome the Prince of life.

"And, behold, there was a great earthquake: for the angel of the Lord descended from heaven." Clothed with the panoply of God, this angel left the heavenly courts. . . .

. . . The soldiers see him removing the stone as he would a pebble, and hear him cry, Son of God, come forth; Thy Father calls Thee. They see Jesus come forth from the grave, and hear Him proclaim over the rent sepulcher, "I am the resurrection, and the life." As He comes forth in majesty and glory, the angel host bow low in adoration before the Redeemer, and welcome Him with songs of praise.[5]

---

* In my book *The Long Road to Armageddon*, I describe in detail the excruciating pain that Jesus suffered from the scourgings, the crown of thorns, and the crucifixion. See Marvin Moore, *The Long Road to Armageddon* (Nampa, ID: Pacific Press®, 2017).

And the apostle John, writing in Revelation, described the rejoicing that all heaven expressed because of the victory that Jesus gained by His death and resurrection:

> "Now have come the salvation and the power
>   and the kingdom of our God,
>   and the authority of his Messiah.
> For the accuser of our brothers and sisters,
>   who accuses them before our God day and night,
>   has been hurled down. . . .
> Therefore rejoice, you heavens
>   and you who dwell in them!
> But woe to the earth and the sea,
>   because the devil has gone down to you!
> He is filled with fury,
>   because he knows that his time is short" (Revelation 12:10, 12).

Satan was a defeated foe, and he knew it. "When he saw Christ come forth [from the tomb] in triumph, he knew that his kingdom would have an end, and that he must finally die."[6]

Praise God that Satan's expectations were shattered—and Jesus' expectations were perfectly fulfilled!

1. Ellen G. White, *The Desire of Ages* (Mountain View, CA: Pacific Press®, 1940), 37.
2. Ellen G. White, "Redemption—No. 2," *Advent Review and Sabbath Herald,* March 3, 1874.
3. White, *Desire of Ages*, 687.
4. White, 782.
5. White, 779, 780.
6. White, 782.

Chapter 7

THE APOSTLES' EXPECTATIONS

I was born in Lima, Peru, the son of Seventh-day Adventist missionary parents. We also spent terms of service in Argentina and Cuba
(before Castro!). After my parents had completed a seven-year term
in Argentina, we all returned to the United States in late 1949 for a
one-year furlough. During that time, we attended the summer 1950
General Conference session in San Francisco, California. I was thirteen
years old at the time, and after more than seventy years, I don't remember
much about the session. But I do know two things: first, throughout the
session, speaker after speaker emphasized the church's mission of taking
the gospel to every nation; and second, I distinctly remember that on
the closing Sabbath, one of the speakers said Jesus' return might happen
before the next session. He certainly hoped so! Of course, as of the
publication of this book, there have been fourteen General Conference
sessions since 1950,* and who knows how many more there will be
before Jesus returns!

This illustrates a characteristic of our human expectation about
Christ's return from the time of the apostles to the present. There's a
dual urgency: Our sense that Jesus is coming soon in light of His Great
Commission compels us on our mission to go into all the world, preach
the gospel, and make disciples of all nations before He returns. Our
sense of mission spurs us to further the spread of the gospel in order to

---

* 1954, 1958, 1962, 1966, 1970, 1975, 1980, 1985, 1990, 1995, 2000, 2005. 2010,
2015.

hasten the return of Jesus. The two motives complement and promote each other. However, Jesus, in His commission, gave us no indication as to *when* He would return. He just promised to be with us "to the very end of the age" (Matthew 28:20); that is, *until* He returns. So, until then, we hope, we expect, we wait—and we continue carrying out the gospel commission.

We find these same two attitudes toward Jesus' second coming in the writings of the New Testament apostles. On the one hand, there was a sense of urgency about preaching the gospel to all the world until He returned, while on the other hand, there was a sense of expectation about His returning within their lifetime.

Proclaiming the gospel

In Jesus' final conversation with His disciples, they asked Him, "Are you at this time going to restore the kingdom to Israel?" (Acts 1:6). He replied, "It is not for you to know the times or dates the Father has set by his own authority" (verse 7). Instead, He told them that "you will receive power when the Holy Spirit comes on you; and you will be my witnesses in Jerusalem, and in all Judea and Samaria, and to the ends of the earth" (verse 8).

Please carefully note the two parts of Jesus' response to His disciples' question. He addressed their expectation first. He said, in essence, "I'm not going to tell you what to expect about the time when I will establish My earthly kingdom. Then He gave them their mission to go and witness for Him in Jerusalem, Judaea and Samaria, and in all the world."

Upon hearing these words and watching His ascension to heaven that immediately followed, the disciples finally realized that Jesus was *not* planning to establish His earthly eternal kingdom anytime soon, and they gave up the idea. Instead, within a few days, they set about to fulfill His command to preach the gospel.

And the result was dramatic! On the day of Pentecost, under the power of the Holy Spirit, Peter preached a bold sermon that resulted in 3,000 people being baptized *that very day* (Acts 2:41). And many more were baptized in the days, weeks, and months that followed. Over the next several decades, the apostles, including Paul, spread the gospel message throughout the Middle East, Europe, and North Africa. From that small beginning, Christianity has been planted on every continent, and it has more adherents than any other religion in the world. So *when* did the apostles think He would come? The New Testament reflects three themes related to this question.

First, Luke's book of Acts makes it very clear that they pushed forward very actively with their mission to proclaim the gospel. Paul especially felt driven to carry the good news about Jesus' life, death, and resurrection to the Gentile world. And Revelation also emphasizes the end-time mission of God's people to proclaim the gospel, especially the three angel's messages in chapter 14.

Second, Paul warned his readers that the end time would bring apostasy, wickedness, and persecution—a theme that is also reflected in John's book of Revelation.

And third, the apostles expressed their expectation that Christ's second coming was imminent, probably within their own lifetimes and those of many of their readers. There was also a great urgency to proclaim the gospel because when that task was completed, Jesus would come. Yes, there was to be a great apostasy, but the apostles thought that also would take place within their own lifetime or shortly thereafter. The idea that the world would continue for almost 2,000 years before Jesus returned was absolutely the farthest thing from the apostles' minds!

It's this third theme—the expectation of Christ's return, probably within the apostles' lifetime—that we will examine in the rest of this chapter.

Christ's return expressed to the Thessalonians

Paul made several comments in his various letters, suggesting that he believed that he and many of the Christians he wrote to would live to see Jesus come. I'll begin with Paul's first letter to the Thessalonians.

First Thessalonians is generally understood by Bible scholars to be the first of the 13 or 14 letters that Paul wrote.* It's addressed to the Christians in the Greek town of Thessalonica. In this letter, Paul made some very specific comments about Christ's second coming. I'm sure you are very familiar with what He said:

> Brothers and sisters, we do not want you to be uninformed about those who sleep in death, so that you do not grieve like the rest of mankind, who have no hope. For we believe that Jesus died and rose again, and so we believe that God will bring with Jesus those who have fallen asleep in him. According to the Lord's word, we tell you that we who are still alive, who are left until the coming of the Lord, will certainly not precede those who have fallen asleep. For the Lord himself will come down from heaven, with a loud command, with the voice of the archangel and with the trumpet call of God, and the dead in Christ will rise first. After that, we who are still alive and are left will be caught up together with them in the clouds to meet the Lord in the air. And so we will be with the Lord forever. Therefore encourage one another with these words (1 Thessalonians 4:13–18).

Reflect with me for a moment on what you would think about the time of Christ's return if you had heard this letter being read in your church on a Sabbath morning. I can tell you what the members of the Thessalonian church thought: they understood Paul to mean that Jesus was coming very soon. After all, didn't Paul refer twice to "*we* who are still alive" at Christ's second coming? And didn't he say that "*we* will be with the Lord forever"? The word *we* would have had to include both Paul and the believers in Thessalonica.†

That, in fact, is exactly what the believers in Thessalonica thought Paul meant. And it lit their enthusiasm about the nearness of Christ's

---

* The author of Hebrews does not identify himself in the book. The number is 14 if Paul was the author; 13 if he wasn't. Bible scholars differ in their views on this topic.

† Some interpreters have suggested that Paul used the word *we* in this passage in a more generic sense, making it applicable to any Christian at any time.

second coming. Wow! Brother Paul assured us that all of us will go to heaven together!

It didn't take long for word of this reaction to reach Paul, who at the time was busy raising up a church in nearby Corinth, and he immediately wrote another letter to the Thessalonian Christians to correct their misunderstanding. We know this letter as 2 Thessalonians. Paul began chapter 2 with these words: "Concerning the coming of our Lord Jesus Christ and our being gathered to him, we ask you, brothers and sisters, not to become easily unsettled or alarmed by the teaching allegedly from us—whether by a prophecy or by word of mouth or by letter—asserting that the day of the Lord has already come" (verses 1, 2). The King James Version says, "that the day of Christ is at hand," meaning that Christ's second coming is near. That, apparently, is the impression that the Thessalonian Christians got from Paul's first letter.

Now notice what Paul said next: "Don't let anyone deceive you in any way, for that day will not come until the rebellion occurs and the man of lawlessness is revealed, the man doomed to destruction" (verse 3). Paul then went on to explain in considerable detail the nature of this rebellion and the fact that the lawless one would bring on some powerful delusions and false miracles to keep those who delight in wickedness from being ready for Christ's return (verses 3–12).

So on the one hand, we have Paul writing very positively about himself and the Thessalonian believers seeing Jesus come in the clouds, while on the other hand, he cautioned them not to become too excited about the soon return of Jesus because a satanic rebellion had to take place first. You and I know that it has taken this satanic rebellion almost 2,000 years to work its way out, and we also know that there is still more to come in our day. However, as I said a moment ago, Paul and the believers in Thessalonica had no idea that there would be a delay of nearly 2,000 years before Jesus showed up to fulfill Paul's prediction in 1 Thessalonians 4!

Christ's return expressed to the Corinthians

First Thessalonians isn't the only place in his epistles where Paul suggested that Christ's second coming was near. In 1 Corinthians 15, Paul said something very similar to what he told the believers in Thessalonica about the immanence of Christ's second coming. Here's what he told them: "Listen, I tell you a mystery: We will not all sleep, but we will all be changed—in a flash, in the twinkling of an eye, at the last trumpet. For the trumpet will sound, the dead will be raised imperishable, and we will be changed" (verses 51, 52).

Paul began by saying, "*We* will not all sleep," by which he meant that "*we* will not all die." In other words, some of the Christians in Corinth, and possibly even Paul himself, would live to see Jesus come. And twice in this passage, Paul said that "*we* will be changed," which would apply to both Paul and all the Corinthian believers, because even if Paul and some of them should die, they would be raised to life at Christ's second coming, and they would all be changed. So, from this passage in 1 Corinthians, it becomes rather obvious that Paul expected Christ's second coming to occur sometime in the next few years.

Numerous explanations have been suggested in an effort to minimize Paul's statements about the nearness of Christ's return in his day, but the fact is that he said what he said. But he made his most specific statement to this effect in his letter to the Christians in Rome.

Christ's return expressed to the Christians in Rome

Now here is how Paul expressed his belief in the immanence of Christ's return in his letter to the Christians in Rome: "And do this [love one another], understanding the present time: The hour has already come for you to wake up from your slumber, because our salvation is nearer now than when we first believed. The night is nearly over; the day is almost here. So let us put aside the deeds of darkness and put on the armor of light" (Romans 13:11, 12).

Paul's statement that the Christians in Rome should awake from their slumber reminds us of Jesus' parable of the ten virgins, who fell asleep as they awaited the arrival of the bridegroom. When the announcement went out that the bridegroom was on his way, only half of the girls had oil in their lamps. The other girls had to go buy some, and when they returned, the door was closed, and they were left out of the wedding banquet. So Paul's advice to "wake up from your slumber" is a clear indication that he believed Christ's coming was near.

And what he said next leaves no doubt about his expectation. He told his readers to wake up from their slumber "because our salvation is nearer now than when we first believed." By "our salvation," Paul didn't mean the salvation that comes when a person accepts Jesus as his or her Savior. He was writing to the Christians in Rome, all of whom would have accepted Jesus as their Savior at some time before Paul wrote to them. Commenting on Paul's words, The *Seventh-day Adventist Bible Commentary* says that "by 'salvation' Paul evidently means the coming of Christ in power and glory."[1] And pay careful attention to what Paul said: "our salvation is *nearer now than when we first believed.*"

Christ's return expressed by the other apostles

Paul wasn't alone in his expectation of Christ's return in his day. James said, "The Lord's coming is near. . . . The Judge is standing at the door!" (James 5:8, 9). Peter said, "The end of all things is near" (1 Peter 4:7). John said, "This is the last hour" (1 John 2:18). And three times in Revelation 22, John wrote that Jesus said, "I am coming soon!" (verses 7, 12, 20). These statements in Revelation have led to the quip that has become common in Adventism, "How soon is soon?" which I adopted as the title of this book.

There are also some more subtle indications that the apostles believed Jesus would return in their day. I will share just one with you. In Philippians 1:6, Paul wrote, "Being confident of this, that he who began a good work in you will carry it on to completion until the day of Christ Jesus." Notice that Paul did not say that "he who began a good work in you will carry it on to completion until the day of your death," which is what actually happened. Rather, at the time Paul wrote to the Christians in Philippi, he still believed that Jesus would come within the lifetime of some of those who were members of that church. That's why he said that "he who began a good work in you will carry it on to completion *until the day of Christ Jesus,*" meaning the day of Christ's return in the clouds of glory to take His redeemed people to heaven.

There can simply be no doubt that all of Christ's apostles—or at least those who wrote books of the New Testament—felt certain that Jesus would return in their day. And not only did they believe this, but they also spoke about it in their inspired writings! And this raises a significant question: aren't inspired authors supposed to tell us the truth about spiritual matters? Why, then, would God's Holy Spirit allow them to mislead their readers into believing that Jesus would return in their day? Jesus Himself told His disciples while He was still with them that "about that day or hour [of His return] no one knows, not even the angels in heaven, nor the Son, but only the Father" (Matthew 24:36). So, why would He inspire His apostles to suggest something that He Himself didn't know at the time He spoke these words?*

Here is one point to consider: Think of the consequences in the minds of the apostles had the Holy Spirit inspired them to say that 2,000 years would pass before He returned! It would have absolutely crushed their evangelistic enthusiasm. Is it possible that God allowed His inspired authors to stress the urgency for the sake of the mission? Note the following comment by *The Seventh-day Adventist Bible Commentary* regarding the inspired authors making these statements about the nearness of Christ's return: "In view of the fact that the Lord did not see fit to reveal the 'day and hour' (Matt. 24:36) of His coming, and urged constant watchfulness upon His followers lest that day come upon them as a 'thief,' what else should we expect but that the NT writers would write of the advent with the overtone of imminency? *This casts no shadow over their inspiration.*"[2]

Paul's final expectation

Eight or nine years after Paul wrote his letter to the Christians in Rome, his expectation of living to see Jesus return had changed drastically. He was now a prisoner, condemned to death by Nero, and he knew that he *would* die before Jesus returned. Here is what he said in his final letter to his good friend Timothy: "The time for my departure is near. I have

---

* I assume that by now Jesus knows the day and hour when He will return.

fought the good fight, I have finished the race, I have kept the faith. Now there is in store for me the crown of righteousness, which the Lord, the righteous Judge, will award to me on that day—and not only to me, but also to all who have longed for his appearing" (2 Timothy 4:6–8).

By "the time for my departure is near," Paul meant, "Now has come the time for my death." And his certainty that Christ would award him a crown "on that day" is another suggestion that he expected Jesus to return on a day beyond his earthly life.

Expectations change as life moves forward. Paul's expectations changed. Millions of Christians since then have had to change their expectations about Jesus' second coming. But two expectations have not changed: First, we know that He *will come back someday*, and that is an expectation that we can all take to the bank! And second, when we die, the next thing we know, Jesus will awaken us at His second coming. Between the time of our death and Jesus' return, we will lie unconscious in the grave. So in a very real sense, the apostles were correct. We can all agree that, from our perspective, Jesus *will* return to take us home to be with Him immediately after we die. And that will seem but an instant of our lifetime!

<hr>

1. Francis D. Nichol, ed., *The Seventh-day Adventist Bible Commentary* (Washington, DC: Review and Herald®, 1957), 6:629.

2. Nichol, 631; emphasis added.

Chapter 8

AUGUSTINE'S EXPECTATION

A ugustine Aurelius, also known as Saint Augustine, was born on November 13, 354. By the time he died on August 28, 430, he had become the most influential theologian in all of Christianity, with the exception of the apostle Paul. Augustine's theological concepts, while modified by the Protestant Reformation, continue to influence both Catholic theology and a significant portion of Protestant Christian teaching to this day. The historian Diarmaid MacCulloch said that "[Augustine's] impact on Western Christian thought can hardly be overstated; only his beloved example, Paul of Tarsus has been more influential, and in any case Westerners have generally seen Paul through Augustine's eyes."[1]

Augustine's early life

Augustine was born in what is now Algeria in North Africa. His mother, Monica, was a devout Christian. When he was eleven years old, his parents sent him to a school in a nearby town, where he learned the Latin language and pagan beliefs and practices. He and his friends lived rather dissolute lives. On one occasion, they stole some fruit from a nearby orchard, not because they were hungry but just because they weren't supposed to! Six years later, at the age of 17, Augustine continued his education at a school in Carthage, and here again, he and his friends lived rather hedonistic lives. He became a Manichaean—a religion that is a combination of Christianity, Gnosticism, and paganism.

After completing his education in Carthage, Augustine moved to

Rome, where he established a school of rhetoric, which is the art of persuasive speech and writing. However, that proved to be a failure, primarily because the students didn't have to pay for their education until they had finished it—and many of them never paid! When an opening for a professor became available at a school of rhetoric in Milan, Italy, Augustine applied for the job and was accepted.

Augustine continued his rather profligate lifestyle throughout his early adult life. He had a couple of concubines, one of whom he was especially fond of and with whom he lived for about fifteen years. They eventually had a son. However, in 385, he broke off his relationship with this woman so he could marry a ten-year-old girl. However, legally he couldn't marry her until she was twelve, so he waited. However, he never married her either because, during those two years, he converted to Christianity and became a Catholic priest. How that came about, I'll explain next.

Augustine, the Christian

After moving to Milan, in due time, Augustine became acquainted with a very friendly man by the name of Ambrose, who was the city's bishop. Ambrose had a profound influence on Augustine. The two connected easily, partly because both were very interested in rhetoric (Ambrose, like Augustine, was a skilled public speaker), and Ambrose became Augustine's spiritual mentor. In due time, Ambrose led Augustine to change from being a Manichaean to being a Christian, and Ambrose baptized him in April 387.

Conversion to Christianity proved to be a profound struggle for Augustine because in the Christian culture of the time, all sexual feelings were considered to be lustful and therefore sinful—and Augustine had enjoyed his sex life! However, as a priest, he was not supposed to get married, so he had to give up all of his lovers and abstain from all sexual activity. He finally surrendered his life totally to God and pledged himself to a life of celibacy. And then, he began his journey toward being one of the most influential theologians in all of Christian history. And this is where we learn of his expectation regarding Christ's second coming.

Augustine's two views of the millennium

In order to understand Augustine's expectations, we need to understand the difference between premillennialism and postmillennialism.
Premillennialists believe that Christ's second coming will happen at the
beginning of the millennium. Seventh-day Adventists are premillennialists because we believe God's people will spend the 1,000-year period
in heaven *after* Christ's second coming. Many Evangelical Protestants
believe Jesus will reign on the earth during the 1,000 years, but either
way, Christ's second coming will happen first and then will come the
millennium. That's why it's called *pre*millennialism.

Postmillennialists believe that the millennium began with Christ's
resurrection and ascension to heaven, and it will continue throughout
Christian history to the second coming of Christ. In other words, Christ
will return at the *end* of the millennium rather than at its beginning.
That's why it's called *post*millennialism.

Early in his Christian life, Augustine was a premillennialist. He
expected Christ to come at the beginning of the millennium. However,
he abandoned that idea because of a group of radical Christians called
Chiliasts who were looking forward to an earthly kingdom in which
the saints would indulge in sensual pleasures that would include both
feasting and sex. So, after his study of the millennium in Revelation
20, Augustine concluded that Christ's millennial kingdom began with
His resurrection and ascension to heaven. He also concluded that this
kingdom would be primarily spiritual in which Christ would reign in
the minds and hearts of Christians. And that part, of course, is very true.
Jesus came to establish a spiritual kingdom, not a political kingdom,
and that spiritual kingdom is supposed to extend to His second coming,
when He will establish His political kingdom alongside the spiritual
kingdom.

Augustine also believed that the mission of the Christian church
during this millennial period was to win the world to Christ, and when
that mission has been largely completed—that is, when most of the world
has adopted the Christian faith—then Jesus will return. This view of the
millennium is still held by postmillennialists to this day: Jesus will return

when the world has been largely converted to Christ. It's obviously been almost 2,000 years since Jesus died, was resurrected, and returned to heaven, so postmillennialists understand the 1,000 years to be symbolic of a long period of time, not a literal 1,000 years.

Augustine's expectation

Once Augustine adopted postmillennialism, he obviously did not expect Christ's second coming to be anywhere close to happening. And the reason for this conclusion is understandable even though it's wrong, being based on erroneous premises. Augustine was born a little over 300 years after Christ ascended to heaven, and by then, it was getting increasingly difficult for Christians to expect Jesus to return in their lifetime. Additionally, Augustine's postmillennial theology caused him to expect the very opposite: he expected the vast majority of the world's human population to be converted before Jesus would return, and nobody knew how long that might take. Augustine's postmillennial theology has had a profound influence on the Christian church, not just theologically but also politically because it led directly to the corrupt power of the papacy during the medieval period. I will now explain why.

By starting the millennium at the beginning of the Christian era, Augustine opened the way for two things: First, there was a reinterpretation of the prophecies of Daniel, especially the prophecy about the great image of Daniel 2. And second, there was a reinterpretation of the church's mission during the millennial period.

Regarding Daniel 2, you are, no doubt, aware that the four metals in that image represent the kingdoms of Babylon, Media-Persia, Greece, and Rome; the feet of iron and clay represent the nations of divided Europe that followed the Roman Empire, and the huge stone that was cut out without hands represents the establishment of God's eternal kingdom.

According to Augustine's postmillennial theory, the stone that crushed the image and became God's eternal kingdom could not represent Christ's *second* coming. Therefore, it must represent the establishment of God's eternal kingdom in this present world at His *first* coming. And, according to his theory, the mission of the church during this millennial period is to win the world to Christ in preparation for His second coming.

Augustine's postmillennial theory dominated Christian theology for about 1,500 years. Both the Catholic Church and Reformed Protestantism (made up largely of Presbyterians, Congregationalists, and a few other smaller denominations) have adopted postmillennialism. I pointed out a page or two back that Augustine considered this earthly kingdom to be spiritual. However, we need to put that in the context of the period of history in which he lived.

It's important to understand that the ideas of church-state separation and freedom of religion that are so familiar to us in today's Western world are fairly new political concepts in world history. The early Christian church arose in a political system in which church and state were closely intertwined. The Roman emperor was considered to be the "god" of the official state religion, and other religions could only practice and proclaim their faith with the permission of the empire. That's "how it was supposed to be" back then.

This is why, when Emperor Constantine converted to Christianity, he had a major role to play in church affairs—and church leaders welcomed him as the leader of their religion. For example, Constantine, the political leader of the Roman Empire, presided at the famous Council of Nicaea, which is especially known for its debate over the Trinity. And it never occurred to either Constantine or the leadership of the church that this was a problem.

Thus, while Augustine considered the millennial kingdom that began with Christ's resurrection and ascension to be spiritual, it was not inconsistent for it also to be very political. And this led straight to the religiopolitical power of the papacy during the medieval period. In fact, our Western concept of religious freedom and separation of church and state was for a long time considered to be anathema by the Catholic Church. Only in the twentieth century did the church acknowledge the principle of religious freedom, and according to Revelation 13, a time is coming when the Catholic Church, along with most Protestants, will revert back to church-state union and the persecution of dissenters.

It's easy to think that these two differing views about the millennium are simply a matter for theologians to debate. However, millennial expectations are closely related to expectations of Christ's return, and, as we have seen, postmillennial theology can have a profound influence on the world's political systems. And, as we shall also see later in this book, they will have a profound influence on the final events of earth's history.

---

1. Diarmaid M. MacCulloch, *Christian History: An Introduction to the Western Tradition* (London: SCM Press, 2012), 106.

Chapter 9

EXPECTATIONS THROUGHOUT CHRISTIAN HISTORY

J esus' promise that He would return, taken together with His statement that "about that day or hour no one knows" (Matthew 24:36; see Acts 1:7), has led to some interesting predictions over the centuries about the time of His second coming. The Wikipedia website, under the heading "List of Dates Predicted for Apocalyptic Events," records almost 200 individuals and groups over the past 2,000 years who have predicted times and dates for the end of the world and the second coming of Jesus. And this list doesn't include the statements of the apostles' expectations that I shared with you in an earlier chapter.

Some of the predictions on this list are based on the possibility of natural events such as major asteroid impacts or alien invasions that would either dramatically alter life on earth or destroy it altogether. However, most of these predictions are about the coming of Christ (Christians), the Messiah (Jews), or the Mahdi (Muslims)—religions that claim Abraham as their founder. Christians and Jews base their claims on the Old and New Testaments and Muslims on the Quran. Some of these predictions are mathematical calculations that are based on the assumed 6,000 years since God created the world.

Polls conducted in 2012 in 20 countries showed that 14 percent of the people in these countries believe the world will end in their lifetime.[1] In this chapter, I will share with you a number of the predictions (expectations) from the past 2,000 years that have to do with the nearness of Christ's second coming, including some that have set dates for that event.

- In about 375, Saint Martin of Tours (a city in France) claimed that the world would end before the year 400. He said, "There is no doubt that the Antichrist has already been born. Firmly established already in his early years, he will, after reaching maturity, achieve supreme power."[2]

- As the year 1000 approached, various Christian clerics predicted it as the date for the millennium to begin or end (depending on whether one accepted a pre- or postmillennial theology). One of these was Pope Sylvester II. As a result, riots allegedly broke out in Europe, and pilgrims traveled to Jerusalem.[3]

- When this prediction failed, some Bible interpreters suggested that the end would occur in 1033, a thousand years after Jesus' death and resurrection.[4]

- Pope Innocent III predicted that the world would end in 1284, 666 years after the rise of Islam in 618. He died in 1216.[5]

- Martin Luther predicted that the world would end no later than the year 1600.[6]

- There was a great deal of anticipation of Christ's second coming among the Anabaptists, who were contemporaries of Luther. A man by the name of Hans Hut predicted that the end would happen on May 27, 1528, and another Anabaptist, Melchior Hofman, said Christ would return in 1533. He claimed that 144,000 people would be saved, while the rest of the world would be consumed by fire.[7]

- In his *Book of Prophecies*, Christopher Columbus predicted that the world would end in 1658.[8]

- Because of the number 666 in the date 1666 and the death of 100,000 Londoners from the bubonic plague and the Great Fire of London, some British Christians known as the Fifth Monarchists believed that the world was about to end.[9]

- The Puritan minister, Cotton Mather, predicted that the world would end in 1697. After this prediction failed, he revised the date to 1736 and then to 1716.[10]

- The Shakers predicted that the world would end in 1792, and when that failed, they changed it to 1794.[11]

- William Miller, the forerunner of the Seventh-day Adventist movement, predicted that Jesus would return sometime between March 1843 and March 1844. When Jesus failed to return during that year, the beleaguered movement rose to the height of enthusiasm by the prediction that Jesus would return on October 22, 1844. When that failed, one of the bitterest disappointments in Christian history gripped the believers.[12] I will have much more to say about this in a later chapter.

- Charles Russell, the forerunner of the Jehovah's witnesses, predicted that Jesus would return in October 1914. He claimed that his prediction was "marked in Scripture."[13]

- The Seventh-day Adventist Margaret Rowen claimed that the world would end at midnight, February 6, 1925.[14]

- Herbert W. Armstrong, the founder of the Worldwide Church of God, assured the members of his church that the rapture would take place in 1936. When that prediction failed, he changed the year to 1943, then 1972.[15]

- Florence Houteff, the leader of the Branch Davidians, predicted that the return of Jesus would begin on April 22, 1959.[16]

- The most persistent predictor of a date for Christ's second coming was the American, Harold Camping, host of the Family Radio broadcast, which was very popular with conservative Christians. He first claimed that the rapture would occur on September 6, 1994. When that failed, he changed the date to September 29 and then to October 2. At this point, he took a break from making predictions, and he began an intense period of Bible study to figure out the truly correct date. Finally, in 2011, he predicted that a "spiritual judgment" would happen on May 21, that year, and this would be followed by the rapture and the end of the world on October 21. These last two predictions generated a great amount of enthusiasm among the followers of Camping's radio program. They covered the United States with preaching and literature, and billboards warning the American people about the coming rapture. Of course, Camping's predictions came to nothing, and he lost all credibility with his followers.[17]

- The French physician and astrologer Nostradamus, who died in 1566, predicted that the "King of Terror" would come from the sky in 1999, with doomsday happening in July that year.[18]
- Jerry Falwell predicted that God's judgment on the world would take place on January 1, 2000, as did Tim LaHaye.[19]
- In late 1976, Pat Robertson predicted that the end of the world would come that year. Later he predicted that the new millennium would begin on the day of earth's destruction—April 29, 2007.[20]
- The psychic and astrologist Jean Dixon predicted that Armageddon would happen on February 4, 1962, a date she later changed to sometime in the year 2020.[21]

This is a sampling of the nearly 200 predictions of the end of the world as we know it over the past 2,000 years, and these expectations were most often generated because of a belief in the second coming of Christ. Yet we wait. Jesus still has not come!

---

1. Chris Michaud, "One in Seven thinks End of World Is Coming: Poll," Reuters .com, May 1, 2012, https://www.reuters.com/article/us-mayancalendar-poll/one-in -seven-thinks-end-of-world-is-coming-poll-idUSBRE8400XH20120501.

2. Otto Friedrich, *The End of the World: A History* (New York: Fromm International Publishing Corporation, 1986), 27.

3. Jason Boyett, *Pocket Guide to the Apocalypse* (Orlando, FL: Relevant Media Group, 2005), 32.

4. Boyett, 32.

5. William P. Lazarus and Mark Sullivan, *Comparative Religion for Dummies* (Hoboken, NJ: Wiley, 2008), 237.

6. Daniel Walther, "Martin Luther and the End of the World," *Ministry* 24, no. 12 (December 1951): 16.

7. Richard Kyle, *The Last Days Are Here Again* (Grand Rapids, MI: Baker Books, 1998), 59.

8. James R. McGovern, ed., *The World of Columbus* (Macon, GA: Mercer University Press, 1992), 17, 36; Reginald Stackhouse, *The End of the World?: A New Look at an Old Belief* (New York: Paulist Press, 1997), 50.

9. Todd Strandberg and Terry James, *Are You Rapture Ready?* (New York City:

Dutton, 2003), 36, 37; Hillel Schwartz, *Century's End: An Orientation Manual Toward the Year 2000* (New York: Doubleday, 1995), 87.

10. Paul Boyer, "Apocalypticism Explained: The Puritans," *Frontline*, PBS, accessed December 9, 2021, https://www.pbs.org/wgbh/pages/frontline/shows/apocalypse/explanation/puritans.html.

11. Richard Abanes, *End-Time Visions* (New York: Four Walls Eight Windows, 1998), 209, 210, 338.

12. "William Miller," Pioneers, Ellen G. White Estate, accessed December 16, 2021, https://whiteestate.org/resources/pioneers/wmiller/.

13. Daniel J. McCoy, ed., *The Popular Handbook of World Religions* (Eugene, OR: Harvest House Publishers, 2021).

14. Michael W. Campbell, "Rowen, Margaret Matilda Wright (1871–1939)," *Encyclopedia of Seventh-day Adventists*, accessed December 16, 2021, https://encyclopedia.adventist.org/article?id=BAVJ&highlight=Margaret|Rowen

15. James Craig Holte, ed., *Imagining the End* (Santa Barbara, CA: ABC-CLIO, LLC, 2020), 217.

16. Jyotsna Sreenivasan, *Utopias in American History* (Santa Barbara, CA: ABC-CLIO, Inc., 2008), 100.

17. Robert D. McFadden, "Harold Camping, Dogged Forecaster of the End of the World, Dies at 92," *New York Times*, December 17, 2013, https://www.nytimes.com/2013/12/18/us/harold-camping-radio-entrepreneur-who-predicted-worlds-end-dies-at-92.html; see also "2012: Apocalypse . . . Not?" *The Blog*, HuffPost, March 5, 2012, https://www.huffpost.com/entry/2012-apocalypse_b_1183943.

18. Everett F. Bleiler, "Nostradamus," *Washington Post*, September 12, 1999, https://www.washingtonpost.com/archive/entertainment/books/1999/09/12/nostradamus/a3fa24e0-55ad-4950-99ac-33da11f3c0b8/.

19. Jason Koebler, "Apocalypse Not: Other Times the World Was Supposed to End—and Didn't," *U.S. News & World Report*, December 20, 2012, https://www.usnews.com/news/articles/2012/12/20/apocalypse-not-other-times-the-world-was-supposed-to-endand-didnt.

20. Koebler, "Apocalypse Not."

21. Jeane Dixon, *The Call to Glory* (New York: Bantam Books, 1971), 170–172.

Chapter 10

EXPECTATIONS OF
THE ADVENTIST PIONEERS BEFORE 1844

The French Revolution, which lasted about ten years, from 1789 to 1799, sparked an intense study of the prophecies of Daniel and Revelation by conservative Protestants in the early years of the 1800s. As LeRoy Froom put it in volume 3 of his four-volume *The Prophetic Faith of Our Fathers*: "The French Revolution was like the explosion of the long-pent-up forces of a volcano. The papal church and state were suddenly torn from their foundation and overwhelmed in the common ruin. The sudden and violent shock sent the Protestant church back to the prophecies."[1]

This sparked a religious awakening and a great interest in the prophecies of Daniel and Revelation and Jesus' return, which lasted through the mid-1800s. Of course, throughout Christian history, beliefs in the nearness of the Second Coming have sparked expectations, but the first half of the 1800s aroused *the* most intense and dramatic expectation in the Christian era up to that time.

The advent awakening
The awakening began in Great Britain and spread rapidly to continental Europe. Prior to this, Protestant Christianity had been buried in *post-millennial* theology, which, as I noted in an earlier chapter, postpones Christ's second coming to an indefinite time, hundreds and perhaps thousands of years in the future. However, in the wake of the French Revolution, conservative Protestants reexamined the significance of *pre*millennial theology, which views the Second Coming as an event

in the near future. In the first four decades of the nineteenth century, more than 100 books on premillennial prophetic interpretation came off the European presses, warning that "the day of the Lord is near—the Judge eternal is coming! Prepare to meet thy God."[2] Expectations were beginning to awaken in God's people—and they would grow!

In Britain, Henry Drummond, a wealthy London banker and a member of Parliament, became a major supporter of this prophetic investigation. He was especially interested in learning about the 2,300-day prophecy of Daniel 8:14 and the 70-week prophecy of Daniel 9:25, and he used his substantial wealth to support those who were studying and proclaiming the news.

In the summer of 1826, Drummond organized a prophetic conference—the first of its kind—that brought together a group of 20 expositors of these prophecies at his luxurious estate at Albury Park in the county of Surrey in southeast England. The attendees were intensely interested in the prophecies of Daniel and Revelation, and they "were anxious to work out satisfying applications for divergent points."[3] These conferences were held every year through 1830. And a general consensus eventually coalesced around the fulfillment of the 2,300 *days* as symbolic of *years* that would end in 1843, 1844, or 1847, depending on when the prophecy went into effect some 450 years before Christ. And back then, the eyes of all these students of prophecy were focused on Turkey and the Ottoman Empire, which they believed would usher in the battle of Armageddon. Froom says that "the apocalyptic vials were believed to have been poured out on Rome in 1798, and the Lord's return was expected in 1847. . . . The current war with Turkey was eagerly watched as an indication of the near approach of the end. The later vials were taken as foreshadowing the proximity of the battle of Armageddon. Prophetic time was believed to have almost expired."[4]

One of the most ardent and active participants in this prophetic revival was Joseph Wolff.[5] He attended at least one of the Albury Conferences, and he traveled extensively throughout Europe, the United States, and Asia. Froom called him "the world's most noted missionary traveler and linguist of his generation."[6] Wolff knew and could speak fourteen languages and was especially fluent in six of them. He also studied Greek, Hebrew, and Latin. In Asia, he preached to Jews, Turks, Hindus, Armenians, and Syrians. In Europe, he spoke before kings and queens as well as the common people, and he also traveled in the United States, where he spoke with American presidents. He spoke before the legislatures of New Jersey and Pennsylvania and even before a joint session of Congress. Wolff was supported financially in all of these travels by the wealthy Henry Drummond. And wherever he went, he proclaimed the soon return of Jesus, which he expected to happen in 1847. He believed that when Jesus returned, He would reign in Jerusalem for 1,000 years.

However, our special interest in this chapter is in the great prophetic awakening in the United States between 1831 and 1844. It began with William Miller, who was the father of the great Advent movement.

William Miller

Many books have been written about the great Advent movement, so obviously, all we can do in this chapter is scan the highlights.

William Miller was born in Pittsfield, Massachusetts, in 1782, and during his adult years, he eventually settled in Low Hampton, New York. From his youth, he was an avid reader, often staying up late at night to read by the light of lit pine knots. In his early twenties, he became a skeptic and joined the Deists, a semi-agnostic "religion," which taught that God created the world and then left it to fend for itself. He concluded that the Bible was filled with contradictions. Nevertheless, he continued in his belief that there was a Supreme Being who manifested Himself in nature and providence. Also, from 1812 to 1814, Miller was a captain of infantry in the United States army. He and his fellow soldiers fought in the war of 1812 against England.

Retiring from military service, Miller retreated to his farm in Low Hampton, where he began attending a Baptist church whose pastor was his uncle, Elisha Miller. One Sunday, in Elisha's absence, he was invited to speak, and partway through the sermon, he broke down and wept at the thought of what Jesus, his Savior, had done for him. He became thoroughly converted and devoted himself to the study of the Bible, especially its prophecies. And he determined to set aside any presuppositions about what the Bible might mean and let it speak for itself. He ultimately came to the conclusion that the time prophecies of Daniel 7, 8, and 9, which were numbered in *days*, should be interpreted as meaning *years*—often called the year-day principle. He was especially impressed with Daniel 8:14, in which Daniel heard a heavenly being say, "Unto two thousand and three hundred days; then shall the sanctuary be cleansed" (KJV). Miller concluded that this time period began in 457 BC and that it would end in AD 1843. He also concluded that the cleansing of the sanctuary represented Christ's second coming when God would cleanse the earth and establish His eternal kingdom.

After fourteen years of study, Miller came under the conviction that he should tell the world what he had learned about the apocalyptic prophecies, especially the 2,300 days of Daniel 8:14 and the 70 weeks of Daniel 9. However, he did not consider himself to be a public speaker, and anxiety about publicly announcing his prophetic conclusions kept holding him back. Finally, however, the conviction became so strong that on August 13, 1831, he came under such a powerful impression that God wanted him to proclaim to the world what he knew that he told Him that if he should receive an invitation to share his convictions publicly, he would do it. And with that, he felt relieved. Surely, God would not require him to preach his convictions about the Second Coming and the end of the world!

Half an hour later, sixteen-year-old Irving Guilford, who was Miller's nephew, knocked on his door. He told Miller that the family's pastor would be away the following Sunday, and would Miller speak at the church in the nearby town of Dresden that day? Miller was shocked and angry for having made that promise to God, but now that he had made it, he had no choice but to obey. And in his own words, when he stood in the pulpit the following Sunday, "As soon as I commenced speaking, all my diffidence and embarrassment were gone, and I felt impressed only with the greatness of the subject, which, by the providence of God, I was enabled to present."[7]

Miller's presentation so impressed his audience that they urged him to speak each evening for the rest of the week and conclude the following Sunday. People came from nearby towns, and a genuine revival took place. Immediately following this series, he was invited by a Baptist preacher in Poultney, Vermont, to present the same series at his church! "Soon he received so many invitations that he could not possibly respond to them all. . . . The Millerite movement was now definitely, though locally, under way."[8] From this small beginning sprang a movement that spread across the entire United States of that time.

The Millerite movement

It's difficult for us, 175 years after the Great Disappointment (as of this writing), to appreciate the profound impact that the Millerite movement had on the American people. As Froom put it in volume 4 of his *Prophetic Faith of Our Fathers*: "Perhaps no phenomenon in the history of American Christianity is comparable to aspects of the great nineteenth-century second advent, or Millerite movement. Without question it made a greater impress upon the consciousness of the American populace within the short space of thirteen years than any other religious development in the annals of the nation."[9]

Miller's movement can be divided into two parts. The first part began in 1831 with his lectures at the church in Dresden, New York, and it extended to 1839; the second phase extended from 1839 to 1844.

The first phase: Preaching in towns and villages. By 1834, Miller's invitations to preach had become so numerous that he had to give up his farming and devote himself entirely to preaching in local churches throughout New England and Eastern Canada. Miller also did a significant amount of publishing during this first phase. It began with a series of eight articles in the Brandon, Vermont, *Telegraph*, which, along with eight additional chapters, he published as a 64-page pamphlet in 1834. Three years later, Miller published a full-fledged book titled, *Evidence From Scripture and History of the Second Coming of Christ, About the Year 1843: Exhibited in a Course of Lectures.*

Commenting on this book, Froom says: "Wherever Miller lectured in person, his printed lectures were now left behind to follow up, amplify, and enforce his oral teaching. . . . And these books began to circulate where Miller had never been in person, creating a wide interest, and preparing the way for his personal appearances."[10]

The second phase: Preaching in the cities. In the autumn of 1839, Miller became acquainted with Joshua Himes, who was the pastor of the Chardon Street Chapel in Boston. Himes brought Miller from small-town presentations to preaching in the large cities of America. "Most eventful of all," Froom said, "Doors were opening everywhere, and the calls for preachers were so many that not half could be filled. So the movement swept on with ever-increasing momentum."[11]

Other developments in the Advent movement

General Conferences. A major contributing factor to the Millerite movement was the impact of sixteen general conferences that were held between 1840 and 1843: five in Massachusetts, one in Maine, five in New York, one in New Hampshire, two in Vermont, and two in Pennsylvania. Twelve of these conferences were held in churches, but four had to be held in halls and auditoriums both because of the large audiences and because of growing hostility toward the movement among the established churches, which increasingly closed their doors to Miller and his associates.

The Broadway Tabernacle that seated 3,500 people was filled, and Philadelphia's Chinese Auditorium that seated 5,000 people was "packed to suffocation."[12] In addition to these larger conferences, smaller local conferences were held throughout Eastern Canada, New England, the Eastern and Middle States, and Ohio in the Midwest.[13] Keep in mind that it was *the expectation of Christ's soon return* that prompted the large crowds.

Camp meetings were another significant factor in the growth of the Millerite movement. These camp meetings were first held in Quebec. In June 1842, Josiah Litch went to Quebec to fulfill a speaking engagement, and large numbers of people came from as far away as 30 or 40 miles to hear the message about Christ's soon return—and this was back in the days before cars and highways and freeways that we are so familiar with. The Millerite leaders had discussed the possibility of experimenting with camp meetings, so Litch decided to try it out right there in Quebec.

Arrangements were made for the land, the word went out, and Litch reported that "waves on waves of people have flowed in upon us, day after day, until our arena within the circle of the tents has been almost crowded with a living mass of beings, eagerly enquiring 'Watchman, what of the night?' "[14] The people in a nearby town were so impressed that they asked for a camp meeting to be held in *their* town! Litch complied, and the result of these camp meetings wasn't just that large crowds heard the message about Christ's soon return; it's that some 500 to 600 people were converted!

The first Millerite camp meeting in the United States was held in East Kingston, New Hampshire, where Froom says, "An 'immense multitude' . . . 'assembled to hear the word of the kingdom.' It was the beginning of a far flung movement which literally 'shook the nation.' "[15] People came from all over New England. Thirty-one camp meetings were held during the summer of 1843, and a total of about 130 were held during 1843 and 1844. People from all Christian denominations came by train, stage, and horse and buggy, with vast crowds thronging each camp. An estimated ten to fifteen thousand people attended that first camp meeting in New Hampshire, and "the interest swept like a rising tide from State to State. So the actual success of the camp meetings led this agency to become a characteristic feature of the Millerite movement."[16]

Here's how Froom described these camp meetings:

The preaching was dynamic and persuasive, and reached the hearts of people. The singing made the camp ring with its fervor, and enforced the oral message. The offerings of gold, silver, and other valuables amounted to one thousand dollars—a large sum for that time, when an average day's work netted only seventy-five cents.

And the parting scene of these camps was unforgettable. United by the bonds of a common faith, and drawn together by a common hope in the soon coming of Christ, they formed a giant circle, hand clasping hand, in solemn leave-taking.[17]

Camp meetings in the cities. Despite their success elsewhere, camp meetings were largely ineffective in reaching the masses in the cities for two reasons. First, churches and even large halls were too small for the enormous crowds. And second, even where venues could have accommodated the crowds, prejudice against the Millerite message increasingly caused doors to be closed to them. To deal with this problem, the Millerite leaders purchased a huge tent with a big pointed top—the largest in the nation—that they could set up on a rented piece of vacant land in a large city. As the crowds grew, the Millerite leaders purchased a forty-foot splice that they could insert into the middle of the tent, making for crowds of 6,000 people. Yet, especially on Sundays, the crowds were so huge that large numbers had to sit outside the tent. The big tent was also set up at the larger camp meetings to accommodate the crowds that attended.

Periodicals were another powerful tool the Millerites used to spread their message. In 1840 and 1841, *Signs of the Times** was the only Millerite publication spreading the message. That increased to six publications in 1842, sixteen in 1843, and twenty-five in 1844, some of which lasted only a few months, but *Signs of the Times* continued from 1840 to 1844 and beyond. These magazines ranged from four-page tabloids that were published daily to others that were published weekly or monthly, and there was a quarterly 148-page scholarly magazine. There was even a special paper for women that was edited by two women preachers!

Disappointment
I pointed out earlier in this chapter that Miller originally predicted that Christ's second coming would take place sometime between the spring

---

* Not to be confused with today's *Signs of the Times*®, which began publication at Pacific Press® in Oakland, California in June 1874.

of 1843 and the spring of 1844, and eventually, a careful study led the Millerite leaders to settle on April 18, 1844, at sundown as the end of the period. However, April 18 came and went, and Jesus did not appear in the skies. The result was more confusion than disappointment. But the Millerites didn't abandon their hope. They referred to this waiting period as "the tarrying time" or "the slumbering time."

Then came Samuel Snow. Snow became a Millerite after reading a second-hand copy of Miller's *Lectures*, and this was followed by a period of intense study of the prophecies and the Hebrew sanctuary services, which together formed the foundation of Miller's conclusion that the 2,300 days would end in early 1844. And Snow became one of the most fervent preachers proclaiming Christ's second coming in 1844.

Snow, however, disagreed with Miller on one important detail. Miller used Pentecost, a spring festival, as the basis for his conclusion that Jesus would come no later than April 18 in the spring of that year. However, Snow noticed that *the cleansing of the sanctuary* in the Hebrew religious year occurred on the Day of Atonement in the *fall*. Therefore, Snow concluded that the correct date for the end of the 2,300 years and Christ's second coming to cleanse the earth by fire would be sometime in the fall of 1844, not the spring. And he used the Karait Jewish calendar to ascertain the exact date for the Day of Atonement, which in 1844 was October 22.

Snow reached this conclusion in February 1844, and he presented it to the other Millerite leaders, but they pretty much turned a cold shoulder. By mid-summer, after the April date had passed, he was getting some positive response, but his real support came from the people at the Exeter camp meeting in New Hampshire, which was held from August 12 to 17. Several speakers made presentations, including Joseph Bates, but the crowd seemed bored and restive.

Then Samuel Snow rode up on horseback, dismounted, and entered the tent where Joseph Bates was speaking. He sat down next to a Mrs. John Couch, who was his sister and the wife of one of the Adventist preachers. In a quiet voice, he explained to her his conviction that the cleansing of the sanctuary of Daniel 8:14 would happen on October 22, the Karait Day of Atonement. Froom said, "Her heart was thrilled with the whispered message. Unable to keep silence, she suddenly rose and in a ringing voice addressed Bates," who was speaking from the pulpit:

> "It is too late [she said] to spend time upon these truths, with which we are familiar." . . .
> . . . "Here is a man with a message from God." . . .
> . . . "Time is short. The Lord has servants here who have meat in due season for his household. Let them speak, and let the people hear them. 'Behold the Bridegroom cometh, go ye out to meet him.' "[18]

Bates replied, "Let him come and deliver his message," and he turned the pulpit over to Snow and sat down.[19] Snow explained his conviction that Jesus would return on October 22, and he backed it up with the biblical evidence he had accumulated. The people were ecstatic. They left the camp meeting and began to spread the October 22 message, and it caught on like wildfire. Suddenly, the Millerite expectations again exploded!

At that camp meeting, Snow made three presentations affirming that Jesus would return on October 22, and he also published them in a four-page magazine called *The True Midnight Cry.* While the major Millerite leaders were hesitant to accept his conclusions, the Millerite public was so energized that his *Midnight Cry* and other publications were distributed by the hundreds of thousands across New England.[20]

Snow's presentations at the Exeter camp meeting launched what has come to be known as the "Midnight Cry." It spread like wildfire. The editor of the *Advent Herald* magazine wrote: "There seemed to be an irresistible power attending its proclamation, which prostrated all before it. It swept over the land with the velocity of a tornado, and it reached hearts in different and distant places almost simultaneously and in a manner which can be accounted for only on the supposition that God was [in] it."[21]

Conferences and camp meetings everywhere proclaimed the message of the Midnight Cry. The various publications soon came around. Miller himself was the last to capitulate. He accepted the October 22 date on October 6. As the day approached, believers abandoned their business affairs, and farmers let their crops spoil in the fields as the people devoted themselves to preparation for the Lord's return. Ellen White commented that "the sincere believers carefully examined every thought and emotion of their hearts. . . . All felt the need of internal evidence that they were prepared to meet the Saviour."[22] The Midnight Cry was a profoundly spiritual movement. Hundreds of people, perhaps thousands, accepted Jesus as their Savior in anticipation of His return.

Hiram Edson, one of the Advent believers, held evening meetings in his home for several days prior to October 22, and on that day, the *Seventh-day Adventist Encyclopedia* says that Edson "invited the people to come to the last meeting, and bade good-by to those who declined, never expecting to meet them again."[23]

The day finally came. The expectation of the Advent believers was at a fever pitch. Enthusiasm was everywhere! This was the day that Jesus would return! When would it happen?

Early morning came. Then late morning. Early afternoon. Late afternoon. The sun went down. Nobody was hungry. No supper. No Jesus.

The clocks chimed eight. Nine. Ten. Eleven. Surely, He would come in this last hour. It was 11:15; 11:30; 11:45; the clock in the front room chimed midnight. No Jesus!

Their expectations were shattered! Here's how Hiram Edson, one of the most committed Advent believers, described their feelings. He said that they looked for the coming of the Lord "until the clock tolled twelve at midnight. Then our disappointment became a certainty. . . . Our fondest hopes and expectations were blasted, and such a spirit of weeping came over us as I never experienced before. It seemed that the loss of all earthly friends could have been no comparison. We wept and wept, till the day dawn."[24]

Hiram Edson's experience was repeated in the lives of thousands of people all over New England. It's estimated that at the time of the Great Disappointment, there were 100,000 to 150,000 Millerite believers in the United States, so let's take the lower figure. A reasonable estimate of the nation's total population at the time would be around 20,000,000 people,[25] making the 100,000 Advent believers about 5 percent of the nation's population. A comparable percentage in 2021, when the nation's population is an estimated 330,000,000,[26] would be 16,500,000 Millerites! That was the power of the Millerite movement in the 1840s!

Now, the point of this entire chapter is expectations. Those who proclaimed the nearness of Christ's coming between about 1800 and 1830 had a mild expectation that Jesus would return by the mid-1840s, but the Millerites had *profound* expectations, and the longer their mission continued, the stronger their expectations grew. By October 22, 1844, their expectation had reached a fever pitch—and their disappointment was just as profound as their expectation!

Yet the interesting thing about this is that Ellen White herself said it was all a part of God's plan! She said that "God designed to prove His people. His hand covered a mistake in the reckoning of the prophetic periods."[27]

Does that surprise you? Then keep reading.

1. LeRoy E. Froom, *The Prophetic Faith of Our Fathers* (Washington DC: Review and Herald®, 1946), 3:263.
2. Froom, *Prophetic Faith of Our Fathers*, 3:266.
3. Froom, 3:449.
4. Froom, 3:450.
5. *Wikipedia*, s.v. "Joseph Wolff," https://en.wikipedia.org/wiki/Joseph_Wolff.
6. Froom, *Prophetic Faith of Our Fathers*, 3:461.
7. Froom, 4:485.
8. Froom, 4:488.
9. Froom, 4:443.
10. Froom, 4:514.
11. Froom, 4:520, 525.
12. Froom, 4:556.
13. Froom, 4:555–557.
14. Froom, 4:642.
15. Froom, 4:643.
16. Froom, 4:645.
17. Froom, 4:646.
18. Froom, 4:811.

19. Froom, 4:811, 812.

20. Froom, 4:801–804.

21. Froom, 4:813.

22. Ellen G. White, *The Great Controversy* (Mountain View, CA: Pacific Press®, 1950), 373.

23. Don Neufeld, ed., *Seventh-day Adventist Encyclopedia* (Hagerstown, MD: Review and Herald®, 1996), 10:412.

24. Arthur L. White, *Ellen G. White: The Early Years*, vol. 1 (Hagerstown, MD: Review and Herald®, 1985), 53.

25. Calculate the estimated population in October 1844 by comparing the 1840 and 1850 census reports and splitting the difference; see "U.S. Population, 1790-2020: Always Growing," U-S-History.com, https://www.u-s-history.com/pages/h980.html.

26. See "U.S. and World Population Clock," Census.gov, https://www.census.gov/popclock/.

27. White, *Great Controversy*, 373.

Chapter 11

THE AFTERMATH OF
THE GREAT DISAPPOINTMENT

The Midnight Cry aroused a profound expectation among those who looked for Jesus to return on October 22, 1844. And then He didn't show up! How do you recover from a failed expectation that's as dramatic as that of the Millerites and which had to be the most widespread and bitterly disappointed expectation in Christian history? I will say this: The recovery took a while. As with any major earthquake, there are always aftershocks. It takes a while for things to settle down. And God understands that. The Great Disappointment was a profound shock to the Advent believers, and shock sends our brains into turmoil and confusion. And God understood that too. In fact, believe it or not, this disappointment was a part of His plan! Speaking of it in her book, *The Great Controversy*, Ellen White commented:

God accomplished His own beneficent purpose in permitting the warning of the judgment to be given just as it was. The great day was at hand, and in His providence the people were brought to the test of a definite time, in order to reveal to them what was in their hearts. The message was designed for the testing and purification of the church. . . .

The disappointment also, though the result of their own misapprehension of the message which they gave, was to be overruled for good. It would test the hearts of those who had professed to receive the warning. In the face of their disappointment would they rashly give up their experience and cast away their confidence in God's word? or would they, in prayer and humility, seek to discern where they had failed to comprehend the significance of the prophecy?[1]

I will briefly explain what I believe was God's intention in allowing His people to experience the Great Disappointment. It was a part of His plan to establish a new movement that would prepare the world for the final crisis, the time of trouble, and Christ's second coming. We, today, know this movement as the Seventh-day Adventist Church, which Revelation 12:17 describes as "the remnant of [the woman's] seed, which keep the commandments of God, and have the testimony of Jesus Christ" (KJV). God knew that several years would pass before the Sabbath-keeping Millerites came to truly understand why God allowed the Great Disappointment to happen, and it would take several more years for Him to send them on the mission that He wanted His remnant church to carry out in the years that followed.

But why did God have to allow the Great Disappointment in order to set in motion His final movement in Christian history? I've pondered that question quite a bit over the years, and my conclusion is that He needed to start it up with a small group of totally dedicated people who would remain faithful to their task and not be sidetracked by other religious forces of their time. And in order to do that, He had to weed out all those persons and organizations that would not be fully committed to the task.

And, indeed, when their expectations were crushed, the vast majority of those who had joined the Millerite movement prior to October 22, 1844, totally rejected William Miller's interpretation of the 2,300 days and the 70 weeks. They went back to their previous lives and lost all interest in Bible prophecy and the coming of Jesus. Obviously, these people would only have watered down God's end-time movement with its commission to prepare the world for Christ's second coming, which is why He weeded them out.

However, the elimination of this vast majority who dropped out on October 23, 1844, was not enough. There were still more that had to be excluded from God's end-time movement. Several groups of people

with varying explanations for the Great Disappointment arose in its
wake. One group claimed that Jesus indeed *had* come on October
22—spiritually, whatever that meant. However, there were two groups
that I will comment on in greater detail. Both of these groups believed
that William Miller's interpretation of the 2,300-day prophecy was
largely correct. However, the first group concluded that October 22 was
the incorrect *date* for the end of the 2,300 days, and they kept pushing
the second coming farther and farther into the future, first into 1845,
then 1846, 1851, 1854, and even into the 1860s and 1870s! Finally,
however, this group faded into oblivion, and they, too, were weeded out
from those who would establish God's end-time movement.

William Miller refused to join this group, even in its earliest stages.
On November 10, 1844, he wrote, "Although I have been twice disappointed, I am not yet cast down or discouraged. . . . My mind is perfectly
calm, and my hope in the coming of Christ is as strong as ever. I have
done only what after years of sober consideration I felt it to be my solemn
duty to do."[2]

The second group could find nothing wrong with Miller's and Snow's
calculation of the date October 22, 1844, for the end of the 2,300 days.
If the 70 weeks and the 2,300 days/years began 457 BC—and they were
convinced that they did—then that time period *had* to end in 1844,
and October 22 was the most logical date. So, they concluded that
their error had to do with the *event* that was supposed to take place on
October 22. Miller also refused to join this group. However, within a
month of October 22, God brought to the fore two ardent Millerites
who explained what actually happened that day. I call them God's spokespersons because, in both cases, the story of what happened provides more
evidence that God was involved. He directed what happened. The first
spokesperson was Hiram Edson.

God's first spokesperson

The interpretation that the 2,300 days of Daniel 8:14 pointed, not to
Christ's second coming but to an *event* that was to happen in heaven
on October 22, 1844, began with Hiram Edson. I pointed out in the

previous chapter that he was the one who brought together a group of Millerite believers in his home on October 22 to await the coming of Jesus. And it was Edson who, following their disappointment, said that "our fondest hopes and expectations were blasted. . . . We wept and wept, till the day dawn."[3]

The morning of October 23, Edson and two friends decided to go visit some of the other Advent believers and encourage them. One of these friends was Dr. Franklin B. Hahn, and the other was a man by the name of O. R. L. Crosier. However, all three of them stayed away from the roads to avoid having to face the taunting crowds, choosing instead to walk through the cornfields. And that also strikes me as the result of divine guidance. God wanted them to avoid the distractions of the crowds that would take their minds away from His leading.

As they were walking through the corn stalks, Edson suddenly stopped. A thought occurred to him, a flash of insight,* that seemed to answer the question that was on all their minds. Here is how he explained it: "Instead of our High Priest *coming out* of the Most Holy of the heavenly sanctuary to come to this earth on the tenth day of the seventh month," Edson realized that "he for the first time *entered* on that day the second apartment of that sanctuary and that he had a work to perform in the Most Holy before coming to this earth."[4] This critical insight laid the first bricks in the foundation of God's end-time movement.

Edson caught up with Hahn and Crosier and shared this fresh insight with them. It immediately made sense to them, too, so the three of them entered into an intense study of the Hebrew Day of Atonement, the cleansing of the sanctuary, and the 2,300 days in Daniel 8:14. Several months later, they published the results of their study in a series of articles in the *Day Dawn*, which was one of several Millerite magazines. And thus began today's Seventh-day Adventist doctrine of the heavenly sanctuary, which gave rise to the doctrine of the investigative judgment about ten years later.

---

* For many years, students of early Adventist history assumed that Edson received a vision in that cornfield. However, a careful examination of the evidence has persuaded most students of Adventist history to conclude that he simply had a flash of insight.

I believe it's very significant that God began explaining the disappointed expectations of the Millerites immediately after their Great Disappointment on October 22, 1844—*the very next morning,* in fact. He revealed the doctrinal/historical issue to His servant Hiram Edson. He made it plain to Edson that the prophecy of the 2300 days and the October 22 date was about an event that took place in heaven, not about Christ's second coming to planet Earth.

God's second spokesperson

Now let's look at God's second spokesperson, who clarified the purpose of the Great Disappointment. The major difference between these two spokespersons is that the first one corrected a misunderstanding about the purpose of the October 22, 1844 date less than 24 hours after the crushing disappointment, and with that, his mission was accomplished. We hear very little about Edson after that. But God's second spokesperson He sent on a lifelong mission. Her name was, at the time, Ellen Harmon.

Sometime in December 1844, Ellen Harmon met with three other women in the home of a Mrs. Elizabeth Haines, who lived in South Portland, Maine. They were confused about the events of the previous several months, and they knelt quietly, earnestly praying for God to give them insight into the meaning of their profound disappointment on October 22. Suddenly, God gave Ellen a vision—her first of many over the next 70 years. "While I was praying," she said, "the power of God came upon me as I had never felt it before. I was wrapped in a vision of God's glory, and seemed to be rising higher and higher from the earth, and was shown something of the travels of the Advent people to the Holy City."[5] Here is how Ellen described this vision:

> I raised my eyes and saw a straight and narrow path, cast up high above the world. On this path the Advent people were traveling to the City, which was at the farther end of the path. They had a bright light set up behind them at the first end of the path, which an angel told me was the Midnight Cry. This light shone all along

the path, and gave light for their feet so they might not stumble. And if they kept their eyes fixed on Jesus, who was just before them, leading them to the City, they were safe.[6]

Ellen said that at the beginning of the path was a large crowd of people making their way up to the New Jerusalem. However, as they ascended, more and more people dropped off the path and descended to the world below. These were the people who rejected the Millerite message and were weeded out. On the other hand, as God's true people kept rising toward the City, they "heard the voice of God like many waters, which gave [them] the day and hour of Jesus' coming. The living saints, 144,000 in number, knew and understood the voice."[7] Ellen's vision concluded with Christ's second coming. The point of this vision was that *God had led His people through the Great Disappointment.* Froom believed that God's purpose in giving Ellen White this vision was

to confirm faith in God's past guidance. Despite their disappointment, there was light in the message—light that would illuminate their entire future pathway. They were not to look to the world. They were traveling on a path to the heavenly city, high above the world. The portrayal did not explain the *nature* of their disappointment; that must come through personal Bible study. But they were not to cast away their confidence, for Jesus was leading them. And they were safe as long, but only as long, as they kept their eyes on Him. They were not to grow weary because the journey was long—"a great way off"—but were to persevere to the end of the road.[8]

Shortly after this, Ellen Harmon received another vision in which she was shown "the disbelief, fanaticism, misrepresentation, and calumny she must meet, but she was told that it was her duty to relate to others what God had shown her."[9] She was shocked! She couldn't imagine herself telling others what God wanted *them* to do and reprimanding *them* when they didn't. She became very depressed and kept to herself for some time. Eventually, however, the conviction that she should tell others what God had shown her became so strong that she ventured out, and so began the seventy-year prophetic ministry of Ellen Gould White.

One of the problems that prompted Ellen Harmon's hesitation to speak publicly about her visions was the fact that at that time, numerous people had arisen who claimed to have received visions, and these, without exception, had been rejected by both Millerites and non-Millerites. And there were those at that time who also rejected her claim to have received visions from God. However, her message resonated with a number of others. It gave them hope in the face of their bitter disappointment.

This movement began with just four people: Edson, Hahn, Crosier, and Harmon. However, others slowly began to join them so that within two or three years, there were approximately 100 people who had become part of God's end-time church. And by this time, both the Sabbath and the biblical teaching about death[10]—two of the foundational teachings of today's Seventh-day Adventist Church—were also a part of the biblical understanding of these 100 individuals. Now please note: God had only about 100 persons who joined His end-time movement *after* October 22, 1844, out of an estimated 100,000-plus Millerites who were part of the movement *before* October 22, 1844! God really did want to purge out the chaff from the wheat!

And thus began the remnant of the woman's offspring (Revelation 12:17), which today has more than 20 million adherents all over the world![11] We today can look back at what those 100 individuals could not possibly have looked ahead and seen. And who knows what the population of this end-time movement will become by the end of the final crisis and the time of trouble, which John described as "a great multitude that no one could count" (Revelation 7:9)! I think we will all be amazed when we get to heaven and can review the record of what developed out of that small beginning of God's end-time movement in the mid-1840s!

I will remind you of several sentences from Ellen White's explanation of the Great Disappointment that I shared with you at the beginning of this chapter:

God accomplished His own beneficent purpose in permitting the warning of the judgment to be given just as it was. The great day was at hand, and in His providence the people were brought to the test of a definite time, in order to reveal to them what was in their hearts. The message was designed for the testing and purification of the church. . . .

. . . It would test the hearts of those who had professed to receive the warning. In the face of their disappointment would they rashly give up their experience and cast away their confidence in God's word? or would they, in prayer and humility, seek to discern where they had failed to comprehend the significance of the prophecy?[12]

I say, Praise God! He truly does work in mysterious ways! So never give up hope just because the past and the future look bleak. Rather, be willing to change your expectations as world events play out. I'm reminded of Ellen White's famous quote, "We have nothing to fear for the future, except as we shall forget the way the Lord has led us, and His teaching in our past history."[13]

Now that we have some background on the Great Disappointment and its aftermath, it's time to talk about the expectations of the Adventist pioneers. I will say this much: They were very biblical. Keep reading!

1. Ellen G. White, *The Great Controversy* (Mountain View, CA: Pacific Press®, 1950), 353, 354.

2. LeRoy E. Froom, *The Prophetic Faith of Our Fathers* (Washington, DC, Review and Herald®, 1954), 4:858.

3. Arthur L. White, *Ellen G. White: The Early Years*, vol. 1 (Hagerstown, MD: Review and Herald®, 1985), 53.

4. Froom, *The Prophetic Faith of Our Fathers*, 4:881; emphasis in the original.

5. White, *Ellen G. White*, 1:53.

6. White, 1:56, 57.

7. White, 1:57.

8. Froom, *Prophetic Faith of Our Fathers*, 4:982.

9. Froom, 4:982.

10. See Donny Chrissutianto, "The Dead Are Really Dead: Revisiting the History of the State of the Dead in Early Adventism, June 2, 2021, https://www.adventistreview.org/2106-50.

11. Andrew McChesney, "Propelled by TMI, Adventist Church Tops 20 Million Members," News, Office of Adventist Mission, accessed December 15, 2021, https://www.adventistmission.org/propelled-by-tmi-adventist-church-tops-20-million-members.

12. White, *Great Controversy*, 353, 354.

13. Ellen G. White, *Last Day Events* (Nampa, ID: Pacific Press®, 1992), 72.

Chapter 12

FROM CONFUSION TO UNITY

The most basic question we need to ask about the Millerite movement, especially the Midnight Cry during its last three months, is whether it was a genuine religious revival or a fanatical deception. Jesus' failure to arrive in the clouds on October 22 would suggest that it was a fanatical deception—and that's how most of the world viewed it, including those on October 23 who abandoned all faith in Miller's message. However, those who remained faithful to the fulfillment of the 2,300 days on October 22 believed that it *was* a genuine revival. They *knew* that God's Spirit had led them and their fellow Millerites. And Seventh-day Adventists, who arose out of that great movement, have held that conviction throughout our 175-year history since that time.

The term *Midnight Cry* comes from the story of the wise and foolish virgins in Matthew 25:1–13. All ten girls had come together to await the coming of the bridegroom, but when he failed to show up as soon as they expected, they fell asleep—all ten of them. Suddenly, "at *midnight* the *cry* rang out: 'Here's the bridegroom! Come out to meet him!' " (verse 6, emphasis added). You know the rest of the story. Five of the girls had extra oil to pour into their lamps, and they were ready to meet the bridegroom and enter into the banquet hall with him. The other five had not come prepared with extra oil, and they had to go out and buy some. But when they returned to the banquet hall, it was too late. The door was shut, and they were not allowed in.

The shut door

The Millerites, as I said, applied the words *midnight cry* from the parable of the ten virgins to their own experience during the last two or three months *before* October 22, 1844. In the parable, the fact that the door was shut to the five foolish virgins when they returned with oil in their lamps meant that their probation had closed. And the Millerites applied the words *shut door* from the parable to their experience *after* October 22.

While Jesus didn't return that day, they felt certain that His coming was nevertheless very near, and probation for the human race had closed. For the next several years, this "shut door" concept was a prominent part of the Millerites' post-October 22 interpretation of the Great Disappointment, including those few who made up the nucleus of the future Seventh-day Adventist Church. However, most of this small nucleus soon came to conclude that probation had not closed for those who had had no part in the Millerite movement. It had closed only for those who had joined the Millerite movement before October 22 but then walked away after the disappointment.

For a few weeks following October 22, Ellen Harmon held to the first view—that probation had closed for the entire world that day. Reflecting on the "shut door" concept years later, in 1883, she wrote, "For a time after the disappointment in 1844, I did hold, in common with the Advent body, that the door of mercy was then forever closed *to the world*."[1] However, for Ellen, this understanding of the shut door lasted only a very short while. She continued:

This position was taken *before my first vision* was given me. It was the light given me of God [in that vision] that corrected our error, and enabled us to see the true position. . . .

I was shown in vision, and I still believe, that there was a shut door in 1844. All who saw the light of the first and second angels' messages and rejected that light, were left in darkness. And those who accepted it and received the Holy Spirit which attended the proclamation of the message from heaven, and who afterward renounced their faith and pronounced their experience a delusion, thereby rejected the Spirit of God, and it no longer pleaded with them.[2]

Two Millerites, Joseph Turner and Apollos Hale, interpreted the disappointment the same way Ellen Harmon did. In the January 1845 issue of a publication called the *Advent Mirror*, they stated that:

> In October 1844 Jesus had gone into a heavenly marriage and . . . soon He would return for the wedding supper at the literal Second Coming. In their understanding, Christ had changed His role from intercessor to king. . . . The October 1844 midnight cry had been the final proclamation of the gospel to the world and . . . "sinners," or the "great mass of the world" could no longer be saved.
>
> [However,] they were very careful to explain that probation had not closed for everyone. Some individuals could still be saved, even those who were outside the Millerite movement, as long as they had not spurned light and were still "subjects of God's mercy."[3]

The idea of the "shut door" that I've shared with you up to this point extended till about 1847. As noted in the last chapter, by this time, the Millerites who would emerge as the Seventh-day Adventist Church had adopted two of the concepts that are a part of our foundational beliefs to this day: the Sabbath and the state of the dead. Joseph Bates was the champion of the Sabbath on the seventh day of the week, and a man by the name of George Storrs introduced the Sabbath-keeping Millerites to the concept of death as a sleep and hell as annihilation rather than eternal punishment. These Sabbath-keeping Millerites also had a basic understanding of the sanctuary and the Day of Atonement in the heavenly sanctuary. And, of course, the premillennial return of Christ was the foundation of the whole Millerite movement, and the budding nucleus of the future Seventh-day Adventist Church maintained that belief as well.

The open door

Sometime during 1847, another view of the shut door began to emerge among the Sabbath-keeping Adventists, though I suggest it could just as well have been called "the open door" view. This understanding was based on God's message in Revelation 3:7, 8 to the church in Philadelphia: "These are the words of him who is holy and true, who holds the key of David. What he opens no one can shut, and what he shuts no one can open. . . . See, I have placed before you an open door." Ellen White had two visions describing this concept, one in 1845 and the other one in 1849. Here is how she described these visions in an 1849 letter:

> I saw [that] the commandments of God and shut door could not be separated. I saw the time for the commandments of God to shine out to His people was when the door was opening in the inner apartment of the heavenly sanctuary in 1844. Then Jesus rose up and shut the door in the outer apartment and opened the door in the inner apartment and passed into the Most Holy Place, and the faith of Israel now reaches within the second veil where Jesus now stands by the ark.
>
> I saw that Jesus had shut the door in the holy place and no man can open it, and that He had opened the door in the Most Holy Place and no man can shut it; and that since Jesus had opened the door in the Most Holy Place the commandments have been shining out and God has been testing His people on the holy Sabbath.[4]

This concept of the door into the Holy Place of the heavenly sanctuary being shut and the door into the Most Holy Place being opened led, in the late 1850s, to the development of the idea of an investigative judgment in the heavenly sanctuary, which has been one of the foundational teachings of Seventh-day Adventists ever since.

Let's now turn to the dual themes of this book: (1) what were the expectations of those Millerites who came through the Great Disappointment still confident that the date October 22, 1844, was correct, and (2) how did that relate to their sense of mission?

Their expectations. We've already seen that, for a few weeks after October 22, Ellen Harmon believed that probation closed for the whole world that day. A few weeks after the Great Disappointment, her first vision changed her mind about the close of probation, but she and the other Millerites who laid the foundation of what would become the Seventh-day Adventist Church continued to expect that Christ's second coming was imminent. For several months, many of them even expected Jesus to return a year later, on October 22, 1845, but they were spared this error when shortly before that date, God told Ellen Harmon that this view was not correct.

Their sense of mission. In the immediate wake of the Great Disappointment, the Millerites were too confused to have a sense of mission, and it took several years for them to even *begin* to realize that God had a work for them to do. It would, in fact, have been premature for these Millerites, no more than two or three years after October 22, 1844, to try to get involved in mission. They did put out a few publications. James White, for example, published 250 copies of a broadside (a single sheet printed on only one side) titled, "To the Little Remnant Scattered Abroad." It included a report of Ellen White's first vision and another vision she had in February 1845. But this was a message to the faithful, not an outreach to the world.[5]

The Adventist pioneers during the late 1840s had major differences of opinion on a variety of biblical teachings, including the popular views of the Sabbath, the state of the dead, and the punishment of the wicked. That's why, at this point, they simply were not prepared to get involved in mission. However, during 1848, they made significant advances toward doctrinal unity through a series of six meetings—Sabbath conferences, they called them—in which forty or fifty Sabbath-keeping Millerites would meet in someone's barn or home to study and sort out their differences. These conferences were held at six New England locations. Our information about them is somewhat limited, and we know more about some of them than we do others. What we do know is that these conferences were crucial for bringing the Sabbath-keeping Millerites onto a united doctrinal foundation. Following is a synopsis of what we know about the locations and discussions of the six Sabbath conferences.

1. *Rocky Hill, Connecticut, April 20–24, 1848.* Fifteen people met on a Friday evening in an unfinished room in the home of a man named Albert Belden. By the next morning, Sabbath, some fifty people crowded into the room. Joseph Bates made a presentation on the Sabbath, urging everyone to keep God's day of rest, and Ellen White reported that "the word had effect to establish those already in the truth and to awaken those who were not fully decided."[6] And her husband, James, said that "God gave His servants the truth in a clear light, and they spoke it with solemn power;" the meeting "was deeply interesting."[7] During the time the Whites were in Rocky Hill, James White mowed hay for 87.5 cents per acre so he c ould earn enough money for him and Ellen to attend the next conference![8]

2. *Volney, New York, August 18, 1848.* The conference in Volney was not nearly as peaceful. This time it was held in the barn of a man named David Arnold. Thirty-five or forty people were present on Friday night, and Joseph Bates preached a strong sermon on the Sabbath. "The brethren are strong on the Sabbath and the shut door [clearly, there were some who still held to that view]. Almost all confessed that they had gained much strength from the meeting. Ellen had two visions at that meeting. She spoke to them with power to their comfort."[9] The next morning thirty-five people showed up, and they were sharply divided. Each person held tenaciously to his or her views and debated them heatedly, claiming that they had biblical evidence to support them. However, the leaders of the group—James and Ellen White and Joseph Bates—told them emphatically that "we had not come so great a distance to hear them, but had come to teach them the truth."[10] Ellen White said,

> These strange differences of opinion rolled a heavy weight upon me, especially as Brother A. spoke of the thousand years being in the past. I knew that he was in

error, and great grief pressed my spirits, for it seemed
to me that God was dishonored. I fainted under the
burden. Brethren Bates, Chamberlain, Gurney, Edson,
and my husband prayed for me. . . . I was soon lost to
earthly things.

My accompanying angel presented before me some of
the errors of those present, and also the truth in contrast
with their errors. That these discordant views, which they
claimed to be according to the Bible, were only according to their opinion of the Bible, and that their errors
must be yielded, and they unite upon the third angel's
message.[11]

Fortunately, they did unite. Ellen White concluded that
"Our meeting ended victoriously. Truth gained the victory."[12]
However, there's more to the story. Most of the people with
these differing views had never met Ellen White before that
meeting, and during the session, God gave them outstanding
evidence of her inspiration and authority as a spokesperson
for Him. You may already be familiar with the story—you
just didn't know that it happened at this small gathering in
Volney, New York. Here's how J. N. Loughborough recounted
the incident in 1885:

As the circumstance was related to me, Sister White,
while in vision, arose to her feet and took [a large, heavy]
family Bible upon her left arm. . . . While holding it
thus, her eyes looking upward and in an opposite direction from the Bible, with her right hand she would turn
from text to text, placing her finger on the text, and
would repeat the same.

Brother Ross looked at many of the texts to see if she
was repeating the one to which she pointed. He or some
of the company looked at them all. In every case she not

only repeated the texts to which she pointed, but she did so while her eyes were fastened upward and in an opposite direction from the Bible. It was these scriptures quoted in this wonderful manner which overthrew the false theories of the Sabbathkeepers assembled at Volney, in August, 1848, and caused them to unite upon the truth.[13]

3. *Port Gibson, New York, August 27, 28, 1848.* This conference was held in the barn of Hiram Edson, who had met with the excited Millerites the evening of October 22, 1844, counting down the hours and minutes till midnight. Here is where they "wept and wept, till the day dawn." It was from this same barn that Edson and his two friends, Franklin B. Hahn and O. R. L. Crosier, had emerged the morning of October 23 and walked through the corn-fields where Edson received his insight that the sanctuary to be cleansed was in heaven. And in this 1848 conference, "harmony prevailed."[14]

4. *Rocky Hill, Connecticut, September 8, 9, 1848.* This conference was also held in the home of Albert Belden, but we know very little about it.

5. *Topsham, Maine, October 22, 1848.* This conference was held in the home of Stockbridge Howland. It was at this conference that the Sabbath-keeping Adventists first discussed the need to publish a paper they could share with both other Millerites and the general public. The paper should document the views that they were bringing together in these Sabbath conferences. However, the attendees had no funds for the project, so they let the issue rest.

6. *Dorchester, Massachusetts, November 18, 1848.* The issue of publishing a paper was again brought up, and the attendees prayed earnestly for light on how to proceed. I will have much more to say about this in the next chapter.

We know that Ellen White had visions at several of these conferences. In fact, I believe that God intentionally gave her these visions as a way to bring the people into unity where otherwise there would almost certainly have been serious conflicts over doctrinal issues. I'm reminded of Paul's words in Ephesians. He said that one of the functions of spiritual gifts, including the gift of prophecy, is

> to equip his people for works of service, so that the body of Christ may be built up until we all reach unity in the faith and in the knowledge of the Son of God and become mature, attaining to the whole measure of the fullness of Christ.
>
> Then we will no longer be infants, tossed back and forth by the waves, and blown here and there by every wind of teaching and by the cunning and craftiness of people in their deceitful scheming. Instead, speaking the truth in love, we will grow to become in every respect the mature body of him who is the head, that is, Christ (Ephesians 4:12–15).

These principles were certainly at work at the Volney, New York, conference of Sabbath-keeping Millerite Adventists! Ellen White's prophetic gift, which was demonstrated in a most remarkable way in the presence of all those present, brought unity where there had been profound disunity.

I cannot emphasize strongly enough the vital significance of these six Sabbath conferences. They laid the vital doctrinal foundation for the Seventh-day Adventist Church that, over the next 175 years, would develop into a global movement with more than 22 million members. This movement has established a global publishing industry, a global health system, and a global educational system that is made up of elementary schools, academies (grades 9–12), colleges, universities, and theological seminaries.

Conclusion

In conclusion, the Great Disappointment was a massive and profoundly emotional event—as I postulated before, it was the most dramatic event in Christian history save for the death of Christ some 1,800 years earlier. But God had a purpose in everything that happened. It was His plan to form a movement that would proclaim the final warning message to the world, but it had to be a movement made up of people who were profoundly loyal to that message. He could never have brought that about through the massive group of Millerites who came together prior to the Great Disappointment.

As I pointed out in the previous chapter, He had to separate the chaff from the wheat. He had to weed out all but those who would be the most devoted, the most committed, to that cause. And He did that through the Great Disappointment. Then, within hours of that disappointment, He set in motion His plan to bring together a tiny nucleus of people— perhaps two or three hundred by the time the 1848 conferences were over—who would join together to create that movement. It began very small—*tiny* would probably be a better word. But like the mustard seed in Jesus' parable, it grew to become a mighty tree where the birds could rest and build their nests (see Matthew 13:31, 32). And, I repeat, today it has spread around the world with 22 million members and is growing.

God truly does work in mysterious ways!

---

1. Ellen G. White, *Selected Messages*, vol. 1 (Washington, DC: Review and Herald®, 1958), 63; emphasis added. The compilers of *Selected Messages* did not give the original source of this quote. Ellen White's grandson, Arthur L. White, who for many years was the director of the Ellen G. White Estate at the General Conference headquarters in Washington, DC, quoted this statement on pages 259–263 of his book, *Ellen G. White: The Early Years, 1827–1862*, volume 1, and he gave the original source as Manuscript 4, 1883.

2. White, *Selected Messages*, 1:63; emphasis added.

3. Joseph Turner and Apollos Hale, "Has Not the Savior Come as the Bridegroom?" *Advent Mirror*, January 1845, in the *The Ellen G. White Encyclopedia*, Denis Fortin and Jerry Moon, eds. (Hagerstown, MD: Review and Herald®, 2013), 1159.

4. Ellen G. White, Letter 5, 1849, in Arthur L. White, *Ellen G. White: The Early Years, 1827–1862* (Hagerstown, MD: Review and Herald®, 1985), 1:262, 263.

5. Arthur L. White, *Ellen G. White*, 1:127.

6. Ellen G. White, in Arthur L. White, 1:137.

7. James White, in Arthur L. White, *Ellen G. White*, 1:137.

8. Fortin and Moon, eds., *The Ellen G. White Encyclopedia*, 307.

9. Arthur L. White, *Ellen G. White*, 1:140.

10. Ellen G. White, in Arthur L. White, 1:141.

11. Ellen G. White, in Arthur L. White, 1:141.

12. Ellen G. White, in Arthur L. White, 1:141.

13. J. N. Loughborough, in Arthur L. White, 1:142.

14. LeRoy E. Froom, *The Prophetic Faith of Our Fathers* (Washington, DC: Review and Herald®, 1954), 4:1023.

Chapter 13

EXPECTATIONS OF
THE ADVENTIST PIONEERS AFTER 1850

E very now and then, I hear someone say, "Don't give me doctrine. Just give me Jesus." And I understand what they mean. They've probably been brought up in a home where they were taught religious ideas without the heartfelt spiritual component. They may even have been subjected to religious rules that were enforced with at least an aluminum fist, if not an iron one.

But anytime you mention the name Jesus, you're getting into doctrine. After all, was He just another human Being, or was He also divine? What was His purpose in coming to our world 2,000 years ago? What did He teach the people He encountered every day? All these questions and more come into play anytime we talk about Jesus—and the answers to these questions are doctrine. There's the doctrine of the Incarnation and the doctrine of the atonement. Even Jesus' crucifixion and resurrection have profound doctrinal and theological implications.

I suggest that doctrine—simple, pure doctrine—is the foundation on which any religious group is formed. In this sense, a religious organization is like any other business: it has to have a purpose, a reason to exist, and it has to have a business plan that corresponds to that purpose. And doctrine is the foundation of a religious organization's purpose—its mission.

The development of mission
I've developed two themes throughout this book: (1) guarding our expectations and (2) guiding our mission. Expectations about Christ's coming prompt our sense of mission and guide it. And this principle is evident

in the six Bible conferences that the early Sabbath-keeping Adventists held in 1848. They laid the doctrinal foundation, the mission statement, of what became the Seventh-day Adventist denomination.

Nor can I emphasize strongly enough the vital contribution that Ellen White had in laying that foundation. In the previous chapter, I shared with you a quote from Ephesians 4 that states the purpose of the gift of prophecy, which is "to equip [God's] people for works of service, so that the body of Christ may be built up until we all reach unity in the faith and in the knowledge of the Son of God and become mature, attaining to the whole measure of the fullness of Christ" (Ephesians 4:12). Ellen White's prophetic gift had a profound influence on bringing unity out of the doctrinal differences that existed in some of those conferences.

And there were other spiritual gifts that Paul mentioned in Ephesians 4:11 that also contributed to bringing unity in those Sabbath conferences. The gift of apostleship—that is, leadership—is evidenced by what Ellen White; her husband, James; and Joseph Bates told the people at the Volney conference, namely, that "we had not come so great a distance to hear them, but had come to teach them the truth."[1] And right there is another of the gifts Paul mentioned in Ephesians—the gift of teaching. All these were at work in those six Sabbath conferences, which brought the Sabbath-keeping Millerites into a unity of mind and purpose.

And this led them to their first small step in the direction of mission. I mentioned in the previous chapter that at their fifth Sabbath conference in Topsham, Maine, the Sabbath-keeping Millerites discussed the *possibility* of publishing a paper, and they even had a season of prayer about the matter with God. But they were mostly poor farmers who didn't have the financial means to support a regularly published paper, so they decided to leave the matter to God and His leading. Then, at the final conference in Dorchester, Massachusetts, they felt such a strong conviction that they should begin to share their message with their fellow Millerites that they again spent some time in a season of prayer, seeking God's guidance.

At that point, Ellen White saw something like the sun glowing before her, and the light kept getting brighter and brighter. Then she heard a voice say to her, "The angels are holding the four winds. . . . The saints are not all sealed.

Yea publish the things thou hast seen and heard, and the blessing of God will attend." "Look ye! That rising is in strength, and grows brighter and brighter."[2]

Ellen White took this to mean that God wanted them to begin publishing to the world what they had come to understand as a result of the Great Disappointment, Hiram Edson's insight in the cornfield, and what they had come to agree upon at their six Sabbath Conferences. So, she told her husband, James, "I have a message for you. You must begin to print a little paper and send it out to the people. Let it be small at first; but as the people read they will send you means with which to print, and it will be a success from the first. From this small beginning it was shown to me to be like streams of light that went clear round the world.[3]

So these few Sabbath-keeping Adventists produced the first copy of a publication called *Present Truth*. The emphasis was on the premillennial second coming of Christ, the Sabbath, the sanctuary, and the Spirit of prophecy. James White found a printer in Middletown, Connecticut, who was willing to print the eight-page tract for a total stranger and await payment until the people to whom the tracts were sent responded with donations to cover the cost. After the pages were printed, James brought them to the home of Albert Belden, and the group of Adventist believers knelt in a circle around them for a season of prayer. "With humble hearts and many tears [the group] besought the Lord to let His blessing rest upon these printed messengers of truth."[4] Then they folded the sheets, wrapped and addressed them, and James White walked to the nearest post office and mailed them. And the people to whom these papers were mailed sent back enough money to cover the printing cost.

After a few issues, the *Present Truth* was replaced by a publication called the *Advent Review*, which became *The Adventist Review and Sabbath Herald*, and which today is simply the *Adventist Review.*

And, so began the movement that in 1863 was formally organized and legally incorporated as the Seventh-day Adventist Church.

On December 25, 1865, Ellen White received a vision about health reform that included the instruction to establish a health-care institution, which the General Conference immediately implemented, and the Health Reform Institution opened its doors the following July. The Health Reform Institution eventually morphed into the Battle Creek Sanitarium, which became one of the best-known medical institutions of its day.

Today, in the United States, the church operates Florida Adventist Hospital in Orlando, Florida; Loma Linda University in Loma Linda, California; and Andrews University in Berrien Springs, Michigan, with the Seventh-day Adventist Theological Seminary on its campus. It also operates eight other colleges and universities in the United States and Canada, two publishing houses—Pacific Press in Nampa, Idaho, and the Review and Herald in Silver Spring, Maryland.

Expectations of these early pioneers

So what were the expectations of this small group of people who formed the nucleus of the Seventh-day Adventist denomination back in the late 1840s and early 1850s? Having come out of the Great Disappointment only five or six years earlier, it's understandable that they would expect Jesus to return within the next few years. We get a clue about this from a remark Ellen White made sometime in 1856: "I was shown the company present at the Conference. Said the angel: 'Some food for worms, some subjects of the seven last plagues, some will be alive and remain upon the earth to be translated at the coming of Jesus.' "[5]

It's obvious from this statement that Ellen White—and by extension her fellow Adventists—believed that Jesus would return within the lifetime of some of those present at that meeting. And the remarkable thing is that this wasn't just Ellen White's opinion. She said it was none other than an angel from heaven who told her that some people in that congregation would live to be translated at Jesus' second coming! However, it has now been more than 160 years since that meeting, and all of those in attendance are awaiting the coming of Jesus in their graves.

Furthermore, throughout her life, Ellen White made many references to the nearness of Christ's return. I will share just a few with you:

- *1862*: "The people of God should awake. Their opportunities to spread the truth should be improved, for they will not last long. . . . The signs of Christ's coming are too plain to be doubted.[6]
- *1872*: "Because time is short, we should work with diligence and

double energy. Our children may never enter college."[7]

- *1876*: "It is really not wise to have children now. Time is short, the perils of the last days are upon us, and the little children will be largely swept off before this."[8]
- *1885*: "In this age of the world, as the scenes of earth's history are soon to close and we are about to enter upon the time of trouble such as never was, the fewer the marriages contracted, the better for all, both men and women."[9]
- *1889*: "The hours of probation are fast closing and the last message of mercy is to be given to the world."[10]
- *1892*: "The time of test is just upon us, for the loud cry of the third angel has already begun in the revelation of the righteousness of Christ, the sin-pardoning Redeemer."[11]
- *1906*: "The end is near; the time is short."[12]
- *1909*: "The message that I am bidden to bear to our people at this time is, Work the cities without delay, for time is short."[13]

Nor was Ellen White alone in her expectation that Christ's second coming was very near. Throughout the remainder of the 1800s, Seventh-day Adventist leaders and laypersons believed the same thing.

1. Ellen G. White, in Arthur L. White, *Ellen G. White: The Early Years, 1827–1862* (Hagerstown, MD: Review and Herald®, 1985), 1:141.

2. LeRoy E. Froom, *The Prophetic Faith of Our Fathers* (Washington, DC: Review and Herald®, 1954), 4:1025.

3. Froom, *The Prophetic Faith of Our Fathers*, 4:1025.

4. Froom, 4:1025.

5. Ellen G. White, *Testimonies for the Church* (Mountian View, CA: Pacific Press®, 1948), 1:131, 132.

6. White, *Testimonies*, 1:260.

7. White, *Testimonies for the Church* (Nampa, ID: Pacific Press®, 2002), 3:159.

8. Ellen G. White, *Last Day Events* (Nampa, ID: Pacific Press®, 1992), 36.

9. White, *Testimonies for the Church* (Nampa, ID: Pacific Press®, 2002), 5:366.

10. White, *Testimonies*, 5:732.

11. White, *Last Day Events*, 37.

12. Ellen G. White, Letter 30, 1906.

13. Ellen G. White, Letter 168, 1909.

Chapter 14

ADVENTIST EXPECTATIONS IN THE LATE 1800S

Most Seventh-day Adventists are aware of our church's understanding of the mark of the beast in Revelation 13:11–18. We believe it is the enforcement of a law by the United States government during the world's final crisis that will require the nation's citizens to observe Sunday as a day of worship, and those who refuse to do so will be refused the right to conduct business, or, as verse 17 says, "they could not buy or sell unless they had the mark [of the sea beast]." We also believe that this will become a global issue that will be enforced by every nation in the world. And the ultimate punishment for those who refuse to worship this beast power will be death (verse 15). This, beyond a doubt, has been our major prediction about the final crisis almost from the beginning of our history.

This understanding of Revelation 13 was first proposed by Joseph Bates in his book *The Sabbath, a Perpetual Sign* that was published in 1847, and it has been our most significant expectation regarding the final crisis ever since.

Ellen White first endorsed this interpretation of the mark of the beast in a pamphlet her husband, James, also published in 1847 titled, *A Word to the Little Flock*. In this pamphlet, "she identified receiving of the mark of the beast as the act of giving up 'God's Sabbath' and keeping 'the Pope's Sabbath.' "[1] And she continued that endorsement throughout her various writings for the rest of her life, especially *Early Writings*, volume 4 of *The Spirit of Prophecy*, and *The Great Controversy*. I will have more to say about Sunday laws in a future chapter of this book.

Sunday laws in the 1880s and 1890s

The point I'm leading up to is that some 40 years after Bates and White first identified the mark of the beast as the legal enforcement of Sunday observance, events began to occur in the United States that seemed to confirm that prediction. Most states in the nation had, for as long as 200 years, had laws prohibiting work on Sunday, though most of those laws had lain dormant during that time. But as Adventism spread around the country, these laws were revived, especially in the South. Between 1885 and 1896, more than 100 Seventh-day Adventists were arrested, fined, and in some cases imprisoned for working on Sunday. Most of these incidents happened in the Southern states at a time when church membership in those states was only a little over 500, and it was only Seventh-day Adventists who were arrested. In some cases, there were non-Adventists working beside the Adventists, but only the Adventists were arrested, tried, and fined or imprisoned!

Given the forty or so years of interpreting Revelation's mark of the beast as Sunday laws, I'm sure you can understand that Seventh-day Adventist church leaders and members everywhere expected that the final crisis and Jesus' second coming were "just around the corner." That's what I would have believed had I lived during those years! Elder I. D. Van Horn, a conference president and a friend of Ellen White, said, "Surely there is no time to idle away, for the [final] crisis is right upon us; the battle must be fought and the victory won."[2]

And the persecution of Seventh-day Adventists for working on Sunday was only the beginning. In 1888 and again in 1889, a United States Senator by the name of H. W. Blair introduced national Sunday law bills in the Senate. Alonzo T. Jones, who by now was well known as one of the major presenters at the 1888 General Conference session in Minneapolis, Minnesota, was a fearless speaker who challenged Blair's bill on the floor of the Senate. And largely as a result of Jones's opposition, these Sunday law bills were defeated in both 1888 and 1889.

So how did Ellen White relate to all these events? What was her expectation? She spoke about it very directly in the following statement from volume 5 of *Testimonies for the Church*, which she wrote sometime in the late 1880s: "The Sunday movement is now making its way in darkness. The leaders are concealing the true issue, and many who unite in the movement do not themselves see whither the undercurrent is tending. Its professions are mild and apparently Christian, but when it shall speak it will reveal the spirit of the dragon. It is our duty to do all in our power to avert the threatened danger. We should endeavor to disarm prejudice by placing ourselves in a proper light before the people."[3]

And on the previous page, she made the following remarkable statement:

> By the decree enforcing the institution of the papacy in violation of the law of God, our nation will disconnect herself fully from righteousness. When Protestantism shall stretch her hand across the gulf to grasp the hand of the Roman power, when she shall reach over the abyss to clasp hands with spiritualism, when, under the influence of this threefold union, our country shall repudiate every principle of its Constitution as a Protestant and republican government, and shall make provision for the propagation of papal falsehoods and delusions, then we may know that the time has come for the marvelous working of Satan and that the end is near.[4]

Ellen White clearly believed that events in the United States at that very time were leading up to the final crisis and Christ's second coming in the immediate future. I think it's safe to say that she expected Jesus to return within her lifetime and the lifetimes of many, if not most, of the other Adventists living back then. Seventh-day Adventist expectations about the nearness of Christ's return during the late 1880s and early 1890s were without a doubt at their highest level since the Great Disappointment.

Interpreting these expectations

Now it's time to raise the same question with respect to Ellen White's expectations that we dealt with in chapter 7 on the expectations of the apostles. In that chapter, I pointed out that Peter, James, John, and Paul all stated very clearly that Jesus' second coming was very near—that if it didn't happen during their lifetime, then surely it would happen shortly thereafter.

For me, the clearest example of this is Paul, who said, "Do this, understanding the present time: The hour has already come for you to wake up from your slumber, because our salvation is nearer now than when we first believed" (Romans 13:11).

And Peter, James, and John chimed in. James, you will recall, said, "The Lord's coming is near. . . . The Judge [Jesus] is standing at the door" (James 5:8, 9). Peter said, "The end of all things is near" (1 Peter 4:7). And John, in Revelation, quoted Jesus Himself saying three times, "Look, I am coming soon!" (twice: Revelation 22:7, 12) and "Yes, I am coming soon" (verse 20).

Therefore, it should come as no surprise that throughout our history, Seventh-day Adventists have expected, or at least hoped, that Jesus would come in their day. And Ellen White backed them up. But why would an inspired writer do that when in the late 1800s, Christ's second coming was still at least 130 years in the future?

As with the apostles' expectations, I believe this is the one area of prophetic writing where God allows His inspired authors to make "a mistake"—and Ellen White was an inspired author. Can you imagine what it would have done to the Millerite Adventists just emerging from the Great Disappointment to know that at least 175 years would go by before Jesus returned? It would have crushed their missionary zeal! And the same thing would have been true had God revealed to Ellen White during the 1880 and 1890 Sunday-law crisis that Christ's second coming was at least 130 years in the future. That's why God allowed her to make the same mistake the apostles made.

I will share with you again a passage in *The Seventh-day Adventist Bible Commentary* that I quoted in chapter 7: "In view of the fact that the Lord did not see fit to reveal the 'day and hour' (Matt. 24:36) of His coming, and urged constant watchfulness upon His followers lest that day come upon them as a 'thief,' what else should we expect but that the NT writers would write of the advent with the overtone of imminency? *This casts no shadow over their inspiration.*"[5]

This paragraph has a special application to the Sunday-law agitation in the 1880s and early 1890s when the expectation was running very high among Adventists that the coming of Jesus was near. And the passage from *Testimonies*, volume 5, that I shared with you a moment ago is a clear indication that Ellen White shared that expectation.

Putting the 1880s and 1890s in perspective

One other factor needs our brief attention with respect to Seventh-day Adventist expectations during the late 1880s and early 1890s. You are, no doubt, aware of the fact that the 1888 General Conference session was held during this period, and it generated a tremendous amount of controversy. E. J. Waggoner made a lengthy presentation on righteousness by faith at a ministerial council that was held prior to the session, and Ellen White gave him her full endorsement. However, because Waggoner based his presentation largely on a reinterpretation of Galatians 3:24, 25 about the law as "our schoolmaster," George Butler, who was the General Conference president at the time, resisted him mightily, as did Uriah Smith and several other prominent leaders in the church. The reason? It contradicted their traditional interpretation of this passage. And their influence clouded the minds of many of the ministers who attended that session. As a result, Waggoner's understanding of righteousness by faith failed to receive the wide reception that it should have.

Because of the resistance by the church's top leadership and the negative influence it had on the church's reception of the message of righteousness by faith, Ellen White wrote the following words in 1893:

> The Lord designed that the messages of warning and instruction given through the Spirit to his people should go everywhere. But the influence that grew out of the resistance of light and truth at Minneapolis, tended to make of no effect the light God had given to his people through the Testimonies. "Great Controversy," Vol. 4 has not had the circulation that it should have had, because some of those who occupy responsible positions were leavened with

the spirit that prevailed at Minneapolis, a spirit that clouded the discernment of the people of God.

The work of opponents to the truth has been steadily advancing while we have been compelled to devote our energies in a great degree to counteracting the work of the enemy through those who were in our ranks. The dullness of some and the opposition of others have confined our strength and means largely among those who know the truth, but do not practice its principles.[6]

Then she went on to explain the delay in Christ's second coming: "If every soldier of Christ had done his duty, if every watchman on the walls of Zion had given the trumpet a certain sound, the world might ere this have heard the message of warning. But the work is years behind. What account will be rendered to God for thus retarding the work?"[7]

In other words, Christ *wanted* to return in the late 1880s and early 1890s, but because of the refusal of many in the church to break out of their apathy and "get on with the program" of preparing themselves and others for His return, it was delayed. That's what Ellen White believed, as did most Adventists at that time.

The problem

I think we need to consider two factors that cause me to question that interpretation. One has to do with the predictions about the end time in Revelation 13, and the other is about what I believe has all along been God's plan for His end-time people, His church, during the final crisis.

Revelation 13. This chapter begins with a beast that rises out of the sea, which Seventh-day Adventists have always identified as the papacy, and I agree with that interpretation. Now notice verse 7, the last half of which says that the papacy will be *"given authority over every tribe, people, language and nation."* In other words, during the world's final crisis, the papacy will achieve global authority.

The second half of chapter 13 introduces us to a beast that rises out of the land, which we have always identified as the United States, and I also agree with that interpretation. And Revelation says that this land beast "exercised all the authority of the first beast on its behalf, *and made the earth and its inhabitants worship the first beast*" (verse 12). And this means that at the end of time, the United States will also unite with the global authority of the papacy.

So there is coming a unified, one-world authority, which, of course, is precisely the ambition of some of the most powerful people in today's world. And, according to Revelation, their ambition will be fulfilled. It will be a global religious power that is intensely hostile to God's end-time people. The dragon will indeed "make war with the remnant of [the woman's] seed" (Revelation 12:17, KJV)—and on a global scale.

And Ellen White supported this concept of an end-time global authority that will enforce the observance of Sunday. In *Early Writings*, her earliest book that describes the final crisis, she said, "Then I saw *the leading men of the earth* consulting together, and Satan and his angels busy around them. I saw a writing, copies of which were scattered in different parts of the land, giving orders that unless the saints should yield their peculiar faith, give up the Sabbath, and observe the first day of the week, the people were at liberty after a certain time to put them to death."[8]

So the opposition that God's people will face in the final crisis will become global. But this didn't happen in the late 1800s because the time had not yet come.

God's plan for His end-time people. To meet the final crisis, I believe God would need a Seventh-day Adventist Church that had developed into a global movement. But we didn't even send out our first foreign missionary, J. N. Andrews, until 1874. Andrews went to Europe, and I believe I'm correct in saying that by the end of that century, we had established a small mission presence in every continent except for Antarctica. But it was barely a start. I believe God's plan was for the Adventist Church to develop a *major* presence on every continent to deal with the final crisis when it comes. And today, we have that global presence. But in the late 1880s, we were just getting started.

I also suggest that we take a moment to compare the methods of travel and communication that existed in the 1880s and 1890s with what is available to us today. Even if everyone back then had been super-faithful to the church's mission, it still remains that crossing the ocean to establish new mission stations was by steamboat, which is far slower than the plane travel we know today. Back then, communication was by letter, which could take weeks to cross the ocean. Today it's via the internet, the World Wide Web, and cell phones, which allow nearly instantaneous communication almost everywhere in the world.

Allow me to share with you a good example of the difference in communication between the late 1800s and today. The US *Signs of the Times®* cooperates with the Australian *Signs of the Times* in the production of our two magazines. We share several of our articles in each issue, which we send to the other country over the internet. Each month, after all the articles for the US issue are edited, a pdf is emailed to the Australian editor in Sydney. He lays out the magazine and sends it back via email for approval. Once the initial draft is approved, he emails it to the magazine's designer, who is several hundred miles away at our Adventist Signs Publishing Company in Warburton in the neighboring state of Victoria. She designs the magazine and sends it back to Pacific Press for approval. It usually takes three or four back-and-forth exchanges, and when she gets final approval, she puts the final draft on Dropbox, which we download at Pacific Press and print in the United States.

This is one small example of the speed with which we can communicate and get our work done globally today, which would have been utterly impossible for our church leaders and workers in the late 1800s and early 1900s.

I propose to you that during the final crisis, God's final warning message will go to the entire world with far greater speed than it ever could have 125 years ago. And I propose that God knew this back in the late 1800s, and He deliberately held off His return until the church could become a global movement with the kind of travel and communication that's available to us today. And He delayed His return until modern science and the technology it has produced could aid us in spreading His end-time message instantly on a global scale.

In fact, I suggest that one of the most powerful means He will use to spread His end-time message will be the very hostile media. They will present our arguments and ridicule and rebut them viciously, but as the saying goes, "You can fool all the people some of the time and some of the people all the time, but you cannot fool all the people all the time." Dedicated Christians of all faiths will recognize the truth, and they will accept it in the face of the fiercest opposition.

I believe the global Seventh-day Adventist movement that has developed since the late 1880s will be absolutely necessary in order for God's people to deal with the coming global opposition that will align against them. And, of course, even with a global movement, we won't be able to deal with the crisis alone. It will take the latter rain power of the Holy Spirit for us to accomplish the task.

I can't tell you how much longer the world is going to continue its present way of life, but I can assure you that our church in the early twenty-first century is much closer to the end than we were at the beginning of the twentieth century.

So while I give due respect to our pioneers in the late nineteenth century and their expectation about the nearness of Christ's return in their day, I am also convinced that all along, it has been God's plan to establish the church's presence all over the globe in a technological setting that will make it possible to proclaim the final warning instantaneously all over the world. It is easy for us to recognize this looking back 125 years. It was impossible for Adventists back then to foresee it looking forward to those same 125 years.

So where do we stand today?
There's still a lot that's unknown to us, especially the time element, but the technological progress in travel and communication during the past 125 years since the late 1800s makes it possible for us to draw fairly realistic expectations about the worldwide finishing of God's work. That would have been impossible for our pioneers in the late eighteenth century to understand, and God also withheld that understanding of the future from our inspired prophet.

The one thing I can assure you of is that Christ's second coming is far closer today than it was back then! So don't give up your expectation of

Christ's soon return. Hang on to it, and let it motivate you to prepare yourself spiritually to deal appropriately with the final crisis when it comes. And let that expectancy motivate you to join your fellow Adventists in spreading the news about Christ's soon coming so that our hope of His return in our day really can happen!

---

1. Dennis Fortin and Jerry Moon, eds., *The Ellen G. White Encyclopedia* (Hagerstown, MD: Review and Herald®, 2013), 961.

2. I. D. Van Horn, "The Michigan State Meeting," *Advent Review and Sabbath Herald*, December 11, 1888, in Arthur L. White, *Ellen G. White: The Lonely Years* (Hagerstown, MD: Review and Herald®, 1984), 419.

3. Ellen G. White, *Testimonies for the Church* (Nampa, ID: Pacific Press®, 2002), 5:452.

4. White, 5:451.

5. Francis D. Nichol, ed., *The Seventh-day Adventist Bible Commentary* (Washington, DC: Review and Herald®, 1957), 6:631; emphasis added.

6. Ellen G. White, "Monday Morning Social Meeting," *General Conference Daily Bulletin*, vol. 5, no. 19, February 28, 1893.

7. White, "Monday Morning Social Meeting."

8. Ellen G. White, *Early Writings* (Washington, DC: Review and Herald®, 1945), 282, 283; emphasis added.

Chapter 15

EXPECTATIONS TODAY

B ack in the late 1970s, my wife, Lois, and I were living in Keene, Texas, and one Sabbath afternoon, we attended a choral concert put on by members of Jerry Falwell's Moral Majority in a town somewhere between Fort Worth and Dallas. The concert, as I recall, was held in a Baptist church, and it was very spiritually uplifting. Lois and I were glad that we attended.

However, there was one aspect of the program that troubled me: the performers stressed the importance of Christians getting involved in America's political process. It wasn't just "get out and vote," which Christians by and large have always encouraged each other to do. This was more like, "Get out and promote your candidate. Support your party (in this case, the Republican Party). Get your church politically active!"

The reason why this troubled me is that I had always believed (and still do) that churches should avoid getting involved in the political process. But that's precisely what this group was encouraging.

Growth of the religious right

This was my introduction to the religious right. And over the years since then, I've watched the religious right become more and more involved in politics, including getting churches and church members politically active. And the religious right has become more and more powerful.

Jerry Falwell's Moral Majority was a significant factor in the election of Ronald Reagan in 1980 and 1984. However, Falwell shut the Moral Majority down in 1989, and the secular press rejoiced. I can remember reading and hearing the enthusiastic proclamation that the religious right was dead, gone, over with! Was the secular left ever wrong! Within less than a year, Pat Robertson, with the aid of his associate, Ralph Reed, started up the Christian Coalition. And Robertson and Reed followed a distinctly different path from Falwell's. Falwell focused his efforts on getting candidates elected to the highest offices in the land: senators, representatives, and presidents. And he had some success. But Robertson and Reed went for the grassroots. They focused their attention on getting conservative Christians elected to *local* offices: mayors, members of city and county councils, and state legislators. Their philosophy was that the power of national political leaders begins at the local level that elects them to office, and if they could grow their political influence at these lower levels, they would end up influencing national politics.

And were they ever right! The Christian Coalition began in about 1990, and for the next four years, Ralph Reed crisscrossed the country, getting Christians and their churches to become involved in local politics and promoting conservative candidates for local and state public offices. At that time, Democrats had held control of both houses of Congress almost continually for the previous 50 years—ever since the time of Franklin D. Roosevelt. But as a result of Robertson and Reed's efforts, in the 1994 midterm election, the Republicans took over the majority in both the United States Senate and the House of Representatives—by wide margins. Suddenly, the religious right, which had been proclaimed dead and buried only a few years earlier, experienced a powerful resurrection that the secular left could no longer ignore. And in 2000, the religious right succeeded in getting George W. Bush elected as president of the United States for his first of two terms.

I watched all of this very carefully because, if you have read my previous books over the years, you know I have always been very interested in end-time events. And as I've reflected on the prophecies of Revelation, especially chapter 13, it has seemed to me that the dominant end-time political powers would be religious, not secular.

The secular Barak Obama won the presidential election in both 2008 and 2012, but then came the stunning 2016 election when Donald

Trump was the victor with the support of the religious right. With the election of Donald Trump, the religious right dominated American politics, though, as you know, the secular left desperately tried to get rid of him, first through the accusation that he was a puppet of the Russians, and when that failed, they tried to remove him through impeachment. But that effort also failed.

As the time for the 2020 election drew near, it seemed to me that Donald Trump held a strong lead over Joe Biden, and I was sure that President Trump would win both the popular vote and the electoral vote, giving the religious right a firm hold on American political power. However, the secular left received the majority of the electors in the 2020 election, putting Joe Biden in office as president of the United States.

Nevertheless, I'm sure you are aware that, for months, there was a huge controversy in the United States over who won the election. The religious right claimed that the secular left won the election through massive fraud, while the left and the media insisted that there was no fraud. There's still a gigantic power struggle going on in America over which side will control the nation's government.

As I write these words, the secular left appears to be in control, but because of Bible prophecy, I suspect that the religious right will come out the ultimate victor. But although I believe they are somewhat more in line with our historic American constitutional principles than the secular left, I don't say this in support of the religious right. I say it because, as I pointed out earlier in this chapter, I believe the end-time political system will be religious, not secular. At least, that's *my* expectation at the time I'm writing these words.

Other trends in today's world

It's time now to take a closer look at some of the other trends in today's United States that are clearly leading us toward the world's final crisis. I'll begin by quoting Jesus' words in Matthew 24:37: "As it was in the days of Noah, so it will be at the coming of the Son of Man." And it's a fact that at least two of the trends in today's world mirror those of the pre-Flood world. Allow me to share them with you.

Pre-Flood marriage. Here's what the first two verses of Genesis 6 tell us: "When human beings began to increase in number on the earth and daughters were born to them, the sons of God saw that the daughters of humans were beautiful, and they married any of them they chose."

At what age do most people today get married? During the latter part of the twentieth century, it was generally in the late teens and early twenties. More recently, it's been the late twenties. In the pre-Flood world, when people lived hundreds of years, the traditional age for marriage may have been considerably later, but either way, they were *young people.* And Genesis says that *the sons of God* were intermarrying with *the daughters of men.* This suggests that the young people who descended from Seth were becoming less and less loyal to their ancestral heritage. They were departing from their religious roots and joining with their secular cousins, the descendants of Cain.

And that's exactly the trend we see taking place in the United States today. For the past several years, the "nones"—people who profess no religious affiliation—have been the fastest-growing segment of the American population. This suggests one fulfillment of Jesus' prediction that "as it was in the days of Noah, so it will be at the coming of the Son of Man" (Matthew 24:37). American society *is* becoming more and more secular, and so is Western civilization as a whole.

Violence. The second similarity between today's Western society and the pre-Flood culture is violence. Genesis 6:11 says that, prior to the Flood, the world "was corrupt in God's sight and was *full of violence*" (emphasis added). And verse 13 says that God declared, "I am going to put an end to all people, for the earth is *filled with violence*" (emphasis added).

Do I have to remind you of the violence that increasingly fills America and our world today? Every week we hear of deranged people going on shooting rampages in public places that kill anywhere from 1 person to as many as 50—and who knows how high that number will grow tomorrow, next month, and next year? Then there are the violent mobs who riot, attack law enforcement officers, and burn and destroy businesses in some of America's major cities.

Three other trends in the United States and Western culture deserve our attention because they are a significant departure from God's Creation mandates. The first is abortion.

Abortion rights. In 1973, the United States Supreme court made a critical moral decision in the *Roe v. Wade* case, which legalized abortion. The court stipulated that "during the first trimester, governments could not prohibit abortions at all; during the second trimester, governments could require reasonable health regulations; [and] during the third trimester, abortions could be prohibited entirely so long as the laws contained exceptions for cases when they were necessary to save the life or health of the mother."[1]

Several states now allow abortion up to the moment of birth, and human life is treated as disposable. Secularists proclaim that a woman has the *right* to *choose* what she will do with her body. I believe that in God's eyes, the woman has a *responsibility* to *protect* the life of her unborn child.

Homosexuality. In Colonial America, homosexual relationships were technically punishable by imprisonment and, in the most extreme cases, by death. These sodomy laws remained on the books of many states throughout the twentieth century until 2003, when the United States Supreme Court ruled in *Lawrence v. Texas* that homosexual acts between consenting adults were not subject to any form of punishment. And I agree with that decision. I don't believe it's the business of the American government to enforce those religious prohibitions. I do, however, support the biblical condemnation of homosexual acts.

In 2015, the Supreme Court decision in *Obergefell v. Hodges* approved homosexual *marriage*. Again, by biblical standards, this is a huge step in the direction of sexual depravity. It is a violation of the Creation mandate that marriage should be between one man and one woman.

And the homosexual community in the United States is determined to abolish all opposition to their so-called civil rights. So, a florist, baker, or photographer who refuses to facilitate their weddings because of conscientious convictions against homosexual marriage is considered to have violated the homosexual couple's civil rights. Thus, religious freedom is called discrimination, and many are taken to court.

Gender confusion. Genesis 1:27 states that "God created mankind in his own image, in the image of God he created them; male and female he created them." Today, in the United States, as well as in many other parts of the Western world, the distinction between male and female is rapidly disappearing. In some places, men can now use women's public restrooms, and women can use men's public restrooms as long as they believe they are the opposite gender from what they were born. The courts have, in some instances, ruled that parents have no right to interfere with the gender choices of their underage children. In Canada, a father who opposed his underage daughter receiving testosterone injections and other gender-altering procedures was jailed, and his daughter was allowed to continue with her gender change!

What difference does it make?

Why do I bring up these issues? Because they are a direct reversal of the Creation mandates: marriage is between one man and one woman, and human beings are created male and female. In today's world, the most basic biblical principles of human life are being ignored and reversed by law.

The seventh-day Sabbath is another Creation mandate, which Seventh-day Adventists have said for the past 175 years will also be violated at the end of time through the enforcement of laws requiring worship on the first day of the week—Sunday.

There's one other development in today's world that I need to bring to your attention: the increasing minimization of religious liberty.

Religious freedom. The First Amendment to the United States Constitution says, "*Congress shall make no law respecting an establishment of religion, or prohibiting the free exercise thereof; or abridging the freedom of speech,* or of the press; or the right of the people peaceably to assemble, and to petition the Government for a redress of grievances."[2]

Throughout American history, this amendment has been esteemed as the most important part of the Bill of Rights, especially as it relates to freedom of religion and freedom of speech. However, the secular left is rapidly challenging that. The civil rights of homosexuals are rapidly taking precedence over the religious rights of those whose conscience cannot allow them to provide services that are directly related to homosexual marriage. In addition to bakers, florists, and photographers targeted by the left for their religious convictions, other professions have also been targeted, such as Christian psychologists and psychiatrists whose conscientious convictions cannot allow them to support homosexuals in their lifestyle.

In the past, all Americans have respected the religious rights of people of faith. But that respect is rapidly disappearing among secular people. Civil rights, while not specifically mentioned in the Bill of Rights, are given greater importance than the religious rights specified in the First Amendment.

And government leaders are battling over the same things. For example, Donald Trump's State Department head, Mike Pompeo, established a Commission on Unalienable Rights in which he named religious and property rights as foremost. However, at his confirmation hearing, Joe Biden's secretary of state, Antony Blinken, claimed that this was Pompeo's way of overriding or neglecting women's reproductive freedom and the rights of LGBTQ people, and he promised to "repudiate those unbalanced views."[3]

Also, in a Senate hearing about the 2021 Equality Act, when Republican senators expressed concern that the wording would undermine religious rights, Democratic Senator Dick Durbin replied that he doubted that the scenarios painted by the Republicans would actually happen. And then he said, "I do believe that people who want to blatantly discriminate and use religion as their weapon have gone too far. We have to have limits on what they can do."[4]

Expectations

So what does this tell us about our expectations for the future? I want to begin by issuing a caution. Every now and then, I hear people say, "Surely, Jesus is going to come in the next five years" or "the next ten years." *We don't know that.* Only God knows when He will return.

Up to this point in the book, I've pointed out time after time when God's people, including His inspired prophets, have proclaimed their expectation that Jesus' second coming would take place "within the next few years." The Millerites even gave it a specific date! But so far, all of these predictions have failed to come to pass. That should give us pause today about proclaiming when Jesus will return or when the final crisis will begin. However, I think it's obvious that the world has changed dramatically since about 1990. As I write these words, both the secular left and the religious right are engaged in a massive fight to the finish.

Revelation 13 suggests to me that the religious right will end up winning the conflict, and the secular left will ultimately join them against God's people. Of course, not knowing the future, I could be wrong. Perhaps the secular left will dominate American politics for a number of years and on into the final crisis, though that also is speculative because the final crisis hasn't started yet. You could call it *my expectation*, based on current political trends in the United States and in light of *my* interpretation of Revelation 13. The fact is that *only God knows the future.*

However, I will make one more suggestion. I suspect that the conflict between religious and secular forces that we see taking place in today's United States will continue until God decides to intervene with a major catastrophe. As I write these words, the COVID-19 pandemic has been raging in the world for a little over a year, and I hear suggestions that even more lethal strains of the disease are in the offing. By the time you read these words, you will know whether that has happened.

However, I don't think coronavirus is the catastrophic event that will usher in the final crisis. I believe it will be far more destructive than that. For example, it could be something on the scale of the Andreas Fault on the West Coast of the United States collapsing, causing massive destruction in San Diego, Los Angeles, San Francisco, and possibly even plunging several miles of coastland into the Pacific Ocean. I'm not saying that that *will be* the natural disaster that ushers in the final crisis. I'm saying I believe it will be something of that magnitude—something that destructive.

I'm reminded of a couple of comments by Ellen White, predicting that a series of natural disasters will initiate the final crisis. One of those statements says, "Transgression has almost reached its limit. . . . We who know the truth should be preparing for what is soon to break upon the world as an overwhelming surprise."[5]

This "overwhelming surprise" could be a natural disaster, but Ellen White didn't say that, so we'll have to wait and see what it is. Here is the other comment about calamities during the final crisis: "So now, a sudden and unlooked-for calamity, something that brings the soul face to face with death, will show whether there is any real faith in the promises of God. It will show whether the soul is sustained by grace."[6]

Again, Ellen White didn't call this calamity a "natural disaster." It could be the sudden outbreak of a global war, or it could be a sudden global economic collapse. Whatever it is, I believe it will initiate the final crisis, which will confront God's people with the need to make some very difficult choices. Until that happens, we wait. And we prepare spiritually. *Please make spiritual preparation for what lies ahead your highest priority!*

---

1. *Wikipedia*, s.v. "Roe v. Wade," last modified November 30, 2021, https://en.wikipedia.org/wiki/Roe_v._Wade.

2. U.S. Const. amend. I § 1; emphasis added.

3. Deirdre Shesgreen, "Blinken Blasts the Trump Administration's 'Unbalanced' Emphasis on Religious Liberty Over Other Human Rights," *USA Today*, April 6, 2021, https://usatoday.com/story/news/politics/2021/03/30/antony-blinken-slams-trumps-heirarchy-human-rights-skewed/4805345001.

4. See Michael Foust, "Opponents of the Equality Act Are Like the KKK, Senator Says: They Used 'Religion as Their Weapon'," *Christian Headlines*, March 18, 2021, https://www.christianheadlines.com/contributors/michael-foust/opponents-of-the-equality-act-are-like-the-kkk-senator-says-they-used-religion-as-their-weapon.html.

5. Ellen G. White, *Testimonies for the Church* (Mountian View, CA: Pacific Press®, 1948), 8:28.

6. Ellen G. White, *Christ's Object Lessons* (Washington, DC: Review and Herald®, 1941), 412.

Chapter 16

SO WHAT LIES AHEAD?

I can remember back in the 1960s and 1970s seeing some very elaborate charts of end-time events that went into great detail about when the latter rain would occur in relation to the loud cry, in relation to the shaking, in relation to the national and international Sunday laws, in relation to spiritualism and Satan's appearance as Christ, in relation to . . . I could keep going, but you get the point. I've never been a fan of these elaborate charts because, to me, they were so much guesswork. I know these events will happen, but trying to arrange them in any kind of future chronological order is simply not possible at this point. We won't know exactly how the end time will work out until it actually happens. However, several major developments will take place during the final crisis, which we can identify, and I will get to that in a moment.

But first, I'd like to look at what God's people in Old Testament times *could* reasonably look forward to—what the ancient Jewish people knew about the coming Messiah. Then I'll compare that with what God's prophecies tell us about the final crisis and the time of trouble to come.

The Old Testament period
Throughout Old Testament history, God's people looked forward to the coming of the Messiah, whom we know as Jesus Christ. They didn't clearly distinguish between the first and second comings of Christ. They thought that when the Messiah came, He would establish His eternal kingdom over the whole earth at that time. Following are some of the prophecies related to the Messiah in the Old Testament.

Adam and Eve. God told Adam and Eve that one of the woman's descendants would strike the serpent on his head, meaning that He would defeat Satan. That was good news. But what else would it have told our first parents about that Descendant, whom we know as Jesus? Not much.

Balaam. Balaam predicted that "a star will come out of Jacob; a scepter will rise out of Israel. . . . A ruler will come out of Jacob" (Numbers 24:17, 19). This is a clear indication that the coming Messiah would be a ruler. Check the rest of the verses in Balaam's prediction, and you will learn that the Messiah would defeat Israel's enemies, and that would be good news. But what else would it have told the Israelites about the coming Messiah? Not much.

Isaiah. Isaiah told the Israelites,

> To us a child is born,
> > to us a son is given,
> > and the government will be on his shoulders. . . .
> He will reign on David's throne
> > and over his kingdom,
> establishing and upholding it
> > with justice and righteousness (Isaiah 9:6, 7).

From this, you could conclude that the Messiah would be born of a woman, which means He would be a human. He would deliver the Israelites from their enemies, and He would establish Israel as an eternal kingdom. And verse 6 would also tell you that the Messiah would be called "Wonderful Counselor, Mighty God, Everlasting Father, Prince of Peace." These words clearly suggest that the Messiah would be a divine Being. Putting these prophecies together provides an important clue about Jesus' dual human and divine nature. But this doesn't provide any of the history of Jesus' life and death that you and I are so familiar with.

The fifty-third chapter of Isaiah also provided the Jews with some very significant information about their coming Messiah:

- Nothing about Him would be particularly attractive, and because of this, He would be despised and rejected (verses 2, 3).
- He would be "pierced for [His people's] transgressions [and] crushed for [their] iniquities" (verse 5). So, in some way, He would take upon Himself the responsibility, the punishment, for their sins (verses 6, 8, 12).
- He would actually die for the sins of His people (verses 10, 12).
- After He died, He would come back to life and be satisfied that His sin offering was worthwhile (verse 11).

Again, these are a few clues about the coming Messiah, but there's so much about Jesus' life, death, and resurrection that you and I are familiar with but of which the people of Isaiah's time knew nothing.

Daniel. Daniel gave a timeline in history about when the people could expect the Messiah to arrive (Daniel 9:25), and the Jews in the early first century AD were very aware of these prophecies. Everyone was expecting the Messiah to appear at any time. But this would have been a very slim slice of knowledge compared to what we, today, know about Jesus.

Micah. Micah foretold the actual town, Bethlehem, in which the Messiah would be born (Micah 5:2), but that's all. He said nothing about Jesus being born in a manger or Joseph and Mary traveling from Nazareth for Him to be born in Bethlehem.

These are among the prophecies about the Messiah that I'm sure Jesus discussed with His two disciples on the road to Emmaus on the afternoon of His resurrection. At that time, they provided enough information about the Messiah's life and His mission that any unprejudiced mind could recognize that Jesus fulfilled them. However, again, what I want you to notice is that they provide almost none of the details about Jesus' life, death, and resurrection that you and I know so well from the New Testament. For example:

- While there's clear evidence that the Messiah would die for human sin, nowhere does the Old Testament say that He would die on a cross.

- It says nothing about Jesus' visit to the temple when He was twelve years old.
- There's nothing about events surrounding His baptism.
- There's not a word about Satan tempting Him in the wilderness.
- There's nothing about the Last Supper or His prayer in Gethsemane.

I could go on and on, but you get the point, I'm sure. The Old Testament gave a broad outline of Jesus' life and death, but it provided very few details. We, on the other hand, know ever so much about the details through the accounts of His life in the four gospels.

The final crisis

Now let's examine what the New Testament and Ellen White tell us about the final crisis and the *second* coming of Jesus Christ, the Messiah. As with the Old Testament prophecies, there are certain things we know will happen, but we don't know the details of how they will actually work out.

I can't set any kind of timeline for when the final crisis will begin, just as I can't set a date for Christ's return. However, I do think we are approaching the final crisis, and I will share with you four general categories of events that can give us a fairly good idea of what to expect in the not-too-distant future. I will also discuss a recent fifth category that has developed in Western society in the past 50 or 60 years that the Bible and Ellen White don't discuss in any detail—but which is shaping up to be a powerful force during the final crisis.

Calamities. The Bible suggests that there will be calamities at the end of time. The seven last plagues are the most striking example, and Jesus' prediction about the falling of the stars is another. We don't get this from Matthew's and Mark's versions of the signs in the heavens, but Luke is very clear that this event or series of events will involve massive calamities. He quoted Jesus saying, "There will be signs in the sun, moon and stars. On the earth, nations will be in anguish and perplexity at the roaring and tossing of the sea. People will faint from terror, apprehensive of what is coming on the world, for the heavenly bodies will be shaken" (Luke 21:25, 26).

The word *anguish* means "this hurts a lot," and *perplexity* means "What do we do now?" And notice that Jesus said that *nations*—that is, *governments*—will be in anguish and perplexity. The world's presidents and prime ministers, their congresses and parliaments, will be at a loss to know how to deal with these signs in the heavens. Jesus went on to say that "people will faint from terror, apprehensive of what is coming on the world, for the heavenly bodies will be shaken." So, the human race will go into a panic when the stars fall, and the sun is darkened. And please note that none of this happened with the Dark Day in 1780 or the falling of the stars in 1833. Therefore, I propose that the ultimate fulfillment of Jesus' signs in the heavens is still in the future.

Ellen White was even more specific about major catastrophes striking our planet during the final crisis: "Calamities will come—calamities most awful, most unexpected; and these destructions will follow one after another."[1] "Cities full of transgression, and sinful in the extreme, will be destroyed by earthquakes, by fire, by flood."[2]

And this is a small sample of comments about calamities during the final crisis that Ellen White wrote about, largely between 1895 and 1905. It's very clear that massive calamities will be one of the characteristics of the final crisis. Some of these will happen before the close of probation, and, of course, the seven last plagues will happen after the close of probation.

I'm going to make a suggestion: I suspect that the final crisis will be initiated by an extreme natural disaster, a global financial meltdown, or a global war. Until one of these three events happens, I would expect the world to go on more or less peacefully, as it has for the past several decades.

Spiritualism. Another major characteristic of the final crisis will be the emergence of spiritualism. Jesus warned His disciples that "false Messiahs and false prophets will appear and perform great signs and wonders to deceive, if possible, even the elect" (Matthew 24:24). Paul said that "the lawless one will be revealed. . . . The coming of the lawless one will be in accordance with how Satan works. He will use all sorts of displays of power through signs and wonders" (2 Thessalonians 2:8, 9). And John said that he "saw three impure spirits . . . demonic spirits that perform signs, and they go out to the kings of the whole world, to gather them for the battle on the great day of God Almighty" (Revelation 16:13, 14).

I'm going to make another suggestion here. I'm sure the coming spiritualistic manifestations will include the seances that are typical of the spiritualism we're accustomed to presently. However, I'm increasingly becoming convinced that a powerful form of spiritualism during the final crisis could be apparitions of supposed aliens communicating with human beings from unidentified flying objects (UFOs). And I believe this especially may happen after the disasters begin to fall. The United States government has been keeping records of UFO sightings for many years, and the government officials who keep track of them are saying that in many cases, these spacecraft are inhabited by alien beings.

Over past decades, most scientists scoffed at the idea of UFOs and at the idea of alien intelligences that might inhabit them. Most probably still do. After all, observation is the basis of all scientific knowledge, and I'm not aware of any scientist ever having seen or communicated with an alien being. Nevertheless, I think the evidence is growing that there *are* intelligent beings onboard these strange objects. As I write these words, the government is preparing to release large amounts of information about UFOs that it has kept secret for many years, and it may have already have happened by the time you read these words. And when these alien beings, which I believe are spirits of demons, inhabiting the UFOs actually make contact with humans, the scientists' eyes and ears will have the evidence that their worldview calls for. Then they will accept the reality of alien inhabitants of UFOs. And when scientists, the source of knowledge in our culture, accept it, the rest of the world will go along.

Could this actually happen, or am I just guessing? Ellen White made one comment that suggests what I've just told you. She said, "Fearful sights of a supernatural character will soon be revealed in the heavens, in token of the power of miracle-working demons."[3] Was she talking about unidentified flying objects? She certainly didn't say so because she had never heard of any such thing as a UFO. But I suspect that God gave her this much of a revelation so that you and I, who have been familiar with the idea of UFOs since the late 1940s, might have some idea about what's coming. That way, we won't be taken by surprise when it happens, and we will be less likely to be deceived.

Persecution of God's people. Revelation 13 is especially clear about the persecution of God's people during the final crisis. Revelation 13 says that the second beast that rises from the earth will "cause all who refused to worship the image [of the beast from the sea] to be killed. It also forced all people, great and small, rich and poor, free and slave, to receive a mark on their right hands or on their foreheads, so that they could not buy or sell unless they had the mark, which is the name of the beast or the number of its name" (verses 15–17).

Revelation 17 begins with a description of a woman who is riding a beast, and I understand this woman to represent the end-time, global religious superpower that includes all or most of the world's religions. Verse 6 says that "the woman was drunk with the blood of God's holy people, the blood of those who bore testimony to Jesus." And verses 12 and 13 describe ten horns on the beast's head that represent ten kings who will "wage war against the Lamb [in the person of His saints], but the Lamb will triumph over them" (verse 14). So, according to both Revelation 13 and 17, God's end-time people can expect bitter persecution—including, in some cases, martyrdom.

And Jesus warned His disciples that "the time is coming when anyone who kills you will think they are offering a service to God" (John 16:2). However, this prediction of Jesus can be applied to various periods, including the Roman government's persecution of God's people during the first three centuries of Christian history, the papal persecution of God's people during the medieval period, the persecution of God's people during the modern era by Hitler's Nazi Germany, Stalin's Communist Russia, and the persecution of Christians today by Muslim forces and by Communist China. And, of course, it can certainly apply to the persecution of God's people during the world's final crisis.

A global superpower. Revelation makes it very clear that there is coming a one-world superpower that will be very religious. This religion will be false, to be sure, but it will be a *religious* authority. Revelation 13:12 says that the beast that rises out of the land, which we understand to be the United States, will exercise "all the authority of the first beast [the sea beast, the papacy] on its behalf, and [make] the earth and its inhabitants *worship* the first beast" (emphasis added).

Two things stand out in this verse. First, the word *worship* suggests that this beast will enforce a religious dogma, and the fact that it makes "*the earth and its inhabitants* worship the first beast" is a clear indication that, in some sense, it will have global authority. And verse 14 supports the conclusion that this beast is a global superpower. It says that the land beast "*ordered* [the inhabitants of the earth] to set up an image in honor of the beast who was wounded by the sword and yet lived" (emphasis added).

Secularism. The fifth category of events that I believe we can count on seeing during the final crisis is those giving rise to secularism. For 200 years, the United States has been a predominantly Christian nation. But a shift toward secularism began in the 1960s. And starting in the early 1990s, it has taken a great leap forward. A religious society is likely to respect freedom of religion, but a secular society doesn't care so much about it. As I pointed out in the previous chapter, Senator Dick Durban recently said, "I do believe that people who want to blatantly discriminate and use religion as their weapon have gone too far. We have to have limits on what they can do."[4]

And that opinion isn't just his alone. His concept of religious freedom mirrors that of the majority of secular people in today's United States. They believe the civil rights of the LGBTQ community take precedence over the religious rights of bakers, florists, and photographers who, because of their religious convictions, do not want to create wedding cakes, floral arrangements, and take photographs for homosexual weddings.

As I'm sure you are aware, there is a great political and cultural divide in the United States in this third decade of the twenty-first century between secularists and religionists. And it would be easy to hope that the religionists will gain back control over the United States government. In fact, I would not be surprised to see this actually happen because my expectation is that the dominant force in society during the final crisis will be religious, not secular, and if this is correct, it suggests that at some point, the religious right will regain its political power. However, don't cheer too loudly over the possibility of the religious right regaining its political authority in the United States. I have been quite concerned about the religious right's "worship" of Donald Trump. Many of them view him almost as a god. In fact, during the first major political rally that he held following his defeat by Joe Biden in the 2020 election, someone created a gold-plated image of Donald Trump and brought it to the rally.

I'm reminded of the early years of Adolph Hitler's tenure in Germany. The country had been devastated by the First World War, the Great Depression had just begun, and the German people were desperate. Hitler came to power in the early 1930s, and the German people all but worshiped him as their savior. But knowing the rest of his history, I think you would agree that we need to be very careful when a large segment of any population practically worships their political leader. I'm not saying that Donald Trump views himself as a god or that any of his devoted followers would call him that, but many of them idolize him. So while one may prefer his loyalty to the American Constitution and his support for the traditional American way of life, given my present conviction that the religious right will be in power during the final crisis, I must recommend caution about supporting Donald Trump and religious conservatives in today's America.

Nonetheless, secularism is a powerful force in today's Western society that we also must take into account as we anticipate the final crisis. As I've already pointed out in this chapter, Revelation 13 makes it clear that religion—worship—will be the dominant issue in the final crisis, both before and after the close of probation. However, secularism will still be a powerful force, and under the influence of spiritualism, it will join hands with the religious leaders against God's people. Religionists will receive the mark of the beast in their foreheads because they believe in it, while secularists will receive the mark in the hand because they have to go along with it in order to buy or sell and, ultimately, save their lives.

The five trends we can expect during the final crisis that I've shared with you in this chapter have already made significant inroads into our Western society, especially in the United States, and I expect to see them develop into full-blown characteristics in the not-too-distant future.

---

1. Ellen G. White, *Evangelism* (Washington, DC: Review and Herald®, 1946), 27.

2. White, *Evangelism*, 27.

3. Ellen G. White, *The Great Controversy* (Mountian View, CA: Pacific Press®, 1950), 624.

4. Rod Dreher, "The War on Religious Liberty," *The American Conservative*, March 17, 2021, https://www.theamericanconservative.com/dreher/the-war-on-religious-liberty.

Chapter 17

FEARFUL END-TIME EXPECTATIONS

Six-year-old Trudy was playing in the yard one afternoon when she felt thirsty, so she ran into the house to get a drink. Several adults were standing around in the kitchen chatting, and one of them turned on the faucet to pour Trudy a glass of water, but the water that came out was a reddish-brown. "Don't drink that water," Trudy's aunt said. "That often happens around here," and she poured the child a glass of orange juice.

Trudy's father said, "Or maybe it's the last days. You know, the seven last plagues—maybe the water's turned to blood."

Everyone chuckled—except for Trudy. Her eyes opened wide, and she said, "Is that really going to happen?"

"That's what the Bible says," one of the adults answered, "but not until the end time."

Trudy went outside, terrified. She had been told that Jesus could return at any time and that the time of trouble would happen just before that. And for the next year, she thought about the awful time of trouble every time she turned on the water faucet to get a drink! In fact, her fear of the end time continued well into her adult life.

Later, when she was in the sixth or seventh grade, her teacher asked the class if they thought they'd be able to remain loyal to Jesus even if they were threatened with death. They all said yes, but Trudy still asked herself, *Could I?* She had heard and read stories about the martyrs for Christ during the Middle Ages, and she wondered whether she could stand the pain of being burned at the stake.

These fears lurked in the back of her mind into her teen years, until finally, one day, she shared them with her father. Her father reminded her of a story about Corrie ten Boom, who as a child lived near Amsterdam, Holland, during the Nazi occupation. Corrie told her father one day that she didn't know whether she could give her life as a martyr if God allowed that to happen.

"Tell me," her father replied, "when you take a train trip from Haarlem to Amsterdam, when do I give you the money for ticket? Three weeks before?"

"No," Corrie replied. "You give me the money for the ticket just before we get on the train."

"And so it is with God's strength," Corrie's father replied. "He will supply the strength you need [to face trial and persecution] just in time."[1]

This illustration helped Trudy to resolve her fear of the end time.

My experience with end-time fears

Unfortunately, Trudy isn't the only Adventist who feels a sense of apprehension as they reflect on the Bible's end-time prophecies, especially as they read Ellen White's account of that difficult period in her book *The Great Controversy.* I will admit to feeling some apprehension about the time of trouble and the bitter persecution God's people will face during that time, but I've learned to temper those fears with Jesus' promise to always be with us "to the very end of the age" (Matthew 28:20); that is, through the time of trouble until His second coming.

During my freshman year in college, I attended two religion classes under the tutelage of Professor Morris Lewis: one on righteousness by faith and the other on Daniel and Revelation. These two classes gave me the foundation for all of my writing during the second half of my life. As most readers of my books and magazine articles know, I write a lot about end-time events, and often I couple them with chapters on how to prepare for those events through the Bible's promises about righteousness by faith.

I was particularly impressed with how deep the feelings of apprehension ran in many Adventist minds when I wrote a piece for the *Adventist*

Today website in response to what I felt were some misunderstandings about the end time in one of their print-magazine articles. I must have received two or three dozen responses to my article, nearly all of which pushed back against my understanding of the end-time crisis because of the fear they all felt about it. And many of them dated those fears back to their childhood when their Adventist parents talked about it. Most of them preferred to just put it out of their minds.

I've learned a couple of good lessons from Trudy's story and the responses of my critics to my post on the *Adventist Today* website. The first lesson is that Adventist parents and elementary school teachers need to be very careful about how they describe the end time to their children. As in Trudy's case, even a casual, offhand remark about the time of trouble can generate a lot of fear in a child's mind. I'm not saying we should avoid talking at all to our children about the time of trouble, but it's imperative that we couple that with the assurance of Jesus' protection during that time. And we also need to be sure our comments are appropriate for the ages of the children. In talking about this with a six-year-old— which was Trudy's age in the incident above—the discussion needs to be much less detailed, and it should always be in the context of God's loving protection.

The second lesson that I learned from the pushback on my *Adventist Today* website article is that fear is a very dysfunctional way to respond to the end-time crisis. I'm reminded of the one-talent man in the parable of the talents. The master, on returning from his journey, asked his three servants what they had done with the talents he had given them. The one-talent man said, "*I was afraid* and went out and hid your gold in the ground. See, here is what belongs to you" (Matthew 25:25; emphasis added).

Please pay careful attention to that response. Fear kept the one-talent man from taking the risk involved in investing his master's money.

And notice the master's reply: "Throw that worthless servant outside, into the darkness, where there will be weeping and gnashing of teeth" (verses 30). Refusal to engage in any necessary activity because of fear is a very dysfunctional response. And that's especially true of the fear we so easily experience when thinking about the challenges of the final crisis and the time of trouble. The right response is not to ignore or deny what inspiration tells us lies ahead. The right response is to deal appropriately with our fear of the future.

Over the years, I've given many seminars on end-time events and how to prepare for them, and there's a question I've at times asked my audience: "Suppose I knew that your house would burn down sometime in the next twelve months. I couldn't give you a date, but I knew beyond a doubt that it would happen. Raise your hand if you would want me to inform you of this coming calamity." Most people raise their hands.

Then I'd ask, "How many people here would *not* want that information?" And a few people would actually raise their hands! It goes beyond my understanding why *anyone* would *not* want that information—*so they could prepare for what was coming!*

I believe that's precisely why God inspired His prophets, especially John, Paul, and Ellen White, to tell us what to expect during the world's final crisis. Paul's comments about the end time are pretty much limited to 1 Thessalonians 5:1–9 and 2 Thessalonians 2:1–12, but his language is very literal. John, writing in Revelation, wrote in more symbolic language, covering the final crisis from Revelation 12:17 to the end of chapter 18. Ellen White, on the other hand, wrote very extensively in very literal language about the world's final crisis, the close of probation, the time of trouble, and Christ's second coming. She devoted chapters 34 to 39 in her book *The Great Controversy* to a description of the final crisis, and chapter 40 is a detailed presentation about Christ's second coming.

There are also scattered chapters and statements about the end-time crisis throughout her extensive writings, one of the most significant of which is a chapter titled "The Coming Crisis" on pages 449 to 454 of volume 5 of *Testimonies for the Church*. And on page 451, she makes a remarkable statement. Please notice the words I have italicized: *when* (three times) and *then* (once) and the last four words, *the end is near*:

By the decree enforcing the institution of the papacy in violation of the law of God, our nation [the United States] will disconnect herself fully from righteousness. *When* Protestantism shall stretch her hand across the gulf to grasp the hand of the Roman power, *when* she shall reach over the abyss to clasp hands with spiritualism, *when*, under the influence of this threefold union, our country shall repudiate every principle of its Constitution as a Protestant and republican government, and shall make provision for the propagation of papal falsehoods and delusions, *then* we may know that the time has come for the marvelous working of Satan and that *the end is near*.[2]

Ellen White did not come close to suggesting a date for Christ's second coming, nor did she give any clue about our ability to set a date when the conditions in the above paragraph have been met. But she did tell us we can know *when the end is near*. None of this has happened yet, but if we can trust the Bible and Ellen White to give us reliable information about the coming final crisis, then when these developments are present in the world, we can put the pieces together and know that Christ's return lies in the near future.

I believe there's a reason why God has given His people at this time in world history the detailed information about the coming crisis that we find in Ellen White's writings: He wants us to understand very clearly what's happening when it happens. He wants us to be able to correctly interpret the events going on in the world around us so that we won't be deceived. A comparison with Christ's final crisis leading up to His crucifixion will clarify what I mean.

From the time they first became acquainted with Him, Jesus' disciples believed that He had come to establish His eternal kingdom on this earth. This belief persisted through His arrest and trial. Judas, who betrayed Him, thought that by doing so, he would influence Jesus to reveal His glory, take control of the Jewish nation, and lead the armies of Israel to victory over the Romans. How wrong they all were! From Gethsemane to His trial and crucifixion, out of that vast crowd—Jewish leaders, Roman governors and soldiers, the rabble that demanded His crucifixion, and even His own disciples—*Jesus was the only One* who understood what was *really* going on. He was the only One who knew that the fate of the world and even of the universe was being decided by the events that were transpiring around them. He was the only One who understood that His trial, crucifixion, and death *had* to take place for the salvation of the human race.

And Jesus *had* to understand this because if He hadn't, He would have given up the conflict, and the whole human race would have been doomed to eternal death.

In the same way, I propose that it will be essential for God's people during the final crisis and the time of trouble to understand what is *really* going on behind the scenes in the world and in the universe. If we don't understand this, we will be much more likely to give up the conflict and yield to the powers that are against us. *That*, I propose, is the reason why Ellen White was given such a detailed description not only of events that will be taking place during the final conflict and the time of trouble but also of the background conditions during those few final years of earth's sin-plagued history. The conflict between good and evil will be reaching its climax.

During the last year of His life on earth, Jesus kept trying to tell His disciples about His coming trial and crucifixion (Matthew 16:21; 26:2), but they would have none of it because it frightened them. It just didn't fit their expectation about the Messiah's role in coming to this world.

The eighteen hours from Gethsemane to His trial and crucifixion were the most critical time in history since Adam and Eve's fall in Eden. The second most critical time will be the world's final crisis, which for us lies in the fairly near future. That's why, throughout our lives, we need to be aware of the broad outline and some of the details of what will happen to God's people during the final crisis. Refusing to be aware of that stressful period because of fear is a straight path to yielding our convictions when the time comes. It is far better for us to understand it and not have it happen during our lifetime than it would be for us to hide our heads in the sand out of fear and have it catch us unaware and unprepared.

---

1. Corrie ten Boom, *Tramp for the Lord* (Fort Washington, PA: CLC Publications, 2010), 125.

2. Ellen G. White, *Testimonies for the Church* (Nampa, ID: Pacific Press®, 2002), 5:451; emphasis added.

Chapter 18

HOW TO PREPARE FOR
THE FINAL CRISIS—PART 1

P reparation for the final crisis and the time of trouble involves three things: First, we need to understand the details of what we can reasonably expect to happen during those months and years. Second, we need to understand our Seventh-day Adventist mission during that time. And third, we need to prepare ourselves spiritually for what lies ahead. In the remainder of this chapter, I will address the first two of these issues: (1) the major details of what we can expect to happen during the final crisis and the time of trouble and (2) the Seventh-day Adventist mission during those two periods. In the final chapter of this book, I'll discuss how you and I can prepare ourselves spiritually for those difficult times.

In the previous chapter, I discussed with you the dysfunctional fear that causes so many good Adventist people to put the whole idea of the final crisis and the time of trouble out of their minds. They don't even want to think about it! And I can appreciate their perspective, given the prediction by both the Bible and Ellen White about the intense persecution God's people will experience during those months and years. At times, I, too, have felt a sense of apprehension about the end-time crisis. However, instead of putting end-time events out of our minds, I suggest that the best way to deal with that fear is to do the opposite: We need to become informed by reading what the Bible and Ellen White tell us about both the final crisis and the time of trouble, and we need to ask God to help us deal with the fear because the surest way to be unprepared for that time when it comes is to allow our fears to keep us from making adequate spiritual preparation ahead of time.

Both the Bible and Ellen White make it clear that the final period in earth's history will be divided into two parts: the final crisis before the close of probation and the great time of trouble after the close of probation.* In the Bible, Revelation 13 and 14 deal with the final crisis before the close of probation, when all human beings are making thefinal decisions that will determine their eternal destiny, and chapters 16 to 18 are primarily about the time of trouble after the close of probation.† So let's talk about the final crisis, and then we'll deal with the time of trouble.

What will happen during the final crisis?

The issue here is what we can reasonably expect to happen during the time when God's people are proclaiming His final warning during the world's final crisis. There obviously isn't time or space in this one chapter to do an in-depth study of Revelation 13 and 14, but I will comment on two issues: Sunday laws and the mission of the Seventh-day Adventist Church during the period when those laws are being enforced.

Sunday laws. Revelation 13 presents us with two beasts. One of them rises from the sea, and the other one rises from the earth. Seventh-day Adventists have traditionally understood the sea beast to be the medieval papacy—a conclusion that I accept, and we have interpreted the second beast to represent the United States of America—a conclusion that I also agree with.

However, there also has to be a sense in which the beast from the sea extends to the final crisis because Revelation 13:12 says that the land beast "exercised all the authority of the first beast on its behalf." This is precisely the relationship between the papacy and the nations of Europe that existed during the medieval period. During that time, the papacy had no army to enforce its dogmas on Europe's citizens. Instead, it depended on Europe's civil powers. Similarly, during the final crisis,

---

* Later in this chapter I will explain the biblical basis for the Seventh-day Adventist belief that human probation will close a short time before Christ's second coming.

† Revelation 18:1–8 is about God's final call to the human race for repentance before the close of probation.

the land beast will *exercise all the authority* of the sea beast on its behalf. This means that the papacy will also have a role to play, not just during the medieval period but during the world's final crisis, and the United States will be its policy enforcer.

The Seventh-day Adventist Bible Commentary, commenting on Revelation 13:12, and specifically the statement that the land beast would exercise "all the power of the first beast before him" (KJV), says, "The first beast, who had been fatally wounded, has come back to life, and is once more active in world affairs. His promoter and agent is the second beast."[1]

Revelation 13 and 14 are about the cooperation between the papacy and the United States in the enforcement of a false form of worship. The word *worship* appears eight times in these two chapters, and of these, seven describe a satanic, false form of worship (Revelation 13:4 [twice], 8, 12, 15; 14:9, 11), and one is about God's true form of worship (Revelation 14:7).

From the very beginning of our movement, Seventh-day Adventists have understood Revelation 14:7 to represent the true worship of God on the seventh-day Sabbath. Verses 6 and 7 are about an angel flying through the air with a message to proclaim to the world, and in the second part of verse 7, the angel says, "Fear God and give him glory, because the hour of his judgment has come. Worship him who made *the heavens, the earth, the sea and the springs of water*" (verse 7). Notice that the last part of Revelation 14:7 is almost a direct quote from the fourth commandment in Exodus 20:

- Revelation 14:7—"Worship him who made the heavens, the earth, the sea and the springs of water."
- Exodus 20:11—"The LORD made the heavens and the earth, the sea, and all that is in them."

This similarity shows that the seventh-day Sabbath is a part of the end-time message God wants His people to proclaim to the world. This has been one of the dominant Seventh-day Adventist understandings about our end-time mission since the beginning of our movement.

Joseph Bates was the first person in Adventism to advance the idea that the mark of the beast will be the legal enforcement of Sunday worship by the laws of the state. He proposed this idea in a pamphlet he published in 1847 titled *The Seventh Day Sabbath, a Perpetual Sign.* By this time, Ellen White and her husband, James, had accepted the Sabbath. She immediately accepted Bates's view of the mark of the beast, and she strongly endorsed it throughout the rest of her prophetic ministry.

Some people have pointed out that Revelation doesn't actually *say* that the mark of the beast is the observance of Sunday when it's enforced by the laws of the state. Of course, it doesn't! Revelation was written in symbolic language several hundred years before the papacy even existed and changed the Sabbath from the seventh to the first day of the week. There's no way John could have known that the mark of the beast two thousand years after his time would have anything to do with a Sabbath-Sunday controversy—especially when that was not even an issue in his day! But if the true worship of God is honoring the Sabbath of the fourth commandment, then the false form of worship elsewhere in Revelation 13 and 14 should be a contrast to that, and the most obvious candidate is Sunday observance.

As I said, Ellen White, guided by the Spirit of inspiration, was very explicit that the mark of the beast is Sunday observance enforced by human laws. This understanding provides the impetus for our mission. And an important part of that mission is the proclamation to the world that the true Sabbath of God is the observance of the seventh day of the week, not the first, because God set that day apart as sacred time.

Our mission. Our understanding of the mark of the beast obviously is not that of the rest of the global Christian community. No other Christian denomination teaches this interpretation of Revelation 13. But if we are correct in our interpretation, they *need* to understand it. This means that it's our responsibility to *warn* them that the mark of the beast is Sunday observance when it's enforced by human laws, and we will have to stand firmly in defense of our Sabbath-keeping principle in the face of the most severe opposition. Ellen White warned:

Men of talent and pleasing address, who once rejoiced in the truth, [will] employ their powers to deceive and mislead souls. They become the most bitter enemies of their former brethren. When Sabbathkeepers are brought before the courts to answer for their faith, these apostates are the most efficient agents of Satan to misrepresent and accuse them, and by false reports and insinuations to stir up the rulers against them.

In this time of persecution the faith of the Lord's servants will be tried. They have faithfully given the warning, looking to God and to His word alone. God's Spirit, moving upon their hearts, has constrained them to speak. Stimulated with holy zeal, and with the divine impulse strong upon them, they entered upon the performance of their duties without coldly calculating the consequences of speaking to the people the word which the Lord had given them. They have not consulted their temporal interests, nor sought to preserve their reputation or their lives. Yet when the storm of opposition and reproach bursts upon them, some, overwhelmed with consternation, will be ready to exclaim: "Had we foreseen the consequences of our words, we would have held our peace." They are hedged in with difficulties. Satan assails them with fierce temptations. The work which they have undertaken seems far beyond their ability to accomplish. They are threatened with destruction. The enthusiasm which animated them is gone; yet they cannot turn back. Then, feeling their utter helplessness, they flee to the Mighty One for strength. They remember that the words which they have spoken were not theirs, but His who bade them give the warning. God put the truth into their hearts, and they could not forbear to proclaim it.[2]

This is one part of the final crisis that some Adventists find to be frightening. However, we need to keep in mind that throughout the ages, there have been times when God's people have similarly faced severe opposition to their beliefs and teachings. Noah was ridiculed for warning his world about a coming Flood. After all, nothing like that had ever happened before—not even a drop of rain! The Israelites were forced into slavery in Egypt, and God called Moses to confront Pharaoh and demand that he let them go; Jeremiah was thrown into a slimy pit for warning the king that if he didn't submit to the Babylonians, they would invade Judah and destroy Jerusalem; Jesus was crucified; the early Christians were persecuted by the Roman government; Protestants were severely persecuted by the papacy during the Middle Ages; Christians today are being persecuted by Communist and Muslim regimes. So what's new about the prediction that persecution lies ahead for Sabbath keepers during the world's final crisis? It's better to be prepared than to pretend that it isn't going to happen!

Spiritualism during the final crisis

The first thing we have to keep in mind as we think about what the Bible and Ellen White tell us about the final crisis and the time of trouble is that this is Satan's last stand. And he knows it. In her chapter "The Time of Trouble" in *The Great Controversy* she says that Satan "numbers the world as his subjects; but the little company who keep the commandments of God are resisting his supremacy. If he could blot them from the earth, his triumph would be complete."[3]

Of course, this is a foolish idea. Satan should know by now that in any contest between himself and Jesus Christ, Jesus always wins, and Satan always loses. And this will also be true of the outcome of the world's final crisis! What he needs to keep in mind is that just because he defeated Adam and Eve doesn't mean he will be able to defeat God's people during the time of trouble! God's people during the final crisis are a unique group. Revelation calls them the 144,000 who have been sealed in their foreheads by God's Holy Spirit, which means that they have developed such an intimate relationship with Jesus that God can trust them to remain loyal under the most severe persecution. They will not be innocently vulnerable the way Adam and Eve were. However, Satan will be determined to defeat them during the time of trouble. This means that they will need a very intimate relationship with Jesus in order to resist the intense pressure that the world will put on them to yield their convictions.

The close of probation. So far as I know, Seventh-day Adventists are the only Christian group that teaches that probation will close shortly before Christ's second coming. Most conservative Christians, if they thought about it, would probably agree that the opportunity to accept Jesus as their Savior will close someday and most would probably say that this will occur at Christ's second coming.

Seventh-day Adventists are unique in teaching that probation will close *prior* to Christ's return. I used to think, like many Adventists, that this concept was based strictly on Ellen White's authority, and that troubled me because our basic beliefs are supposed to be grounded in the Bible. It's true, of course, that she had a lot to say about this topic. However, she didn't create it. When I began a search in Revelation for the close of probation, it didn't take me long to find significant biblical evidence to support it.

Revelation 15 is very clear. The chapter begins with the song of Moses in verses 1–4. Then come seven angels who are "dressed in clean, shining linen and [wear] golden sashes around their chests" (verse 6). They are given the seven bowls filled with God's wrath, and verse 8 says that "the temple was filled with smoke from the glory of God and from his power, and no one could enter the temple until the seven plagues of the seven angels were completed." The words "no one could enter the temple" would have to include Jesus Christ, our heavenly Mediator. His mediatorial ministry is finished, meaning probation has closed. Once His mediatorial ministry has ceased, all those who have committed their lives to Jesus prior to that time are guaranteed their eternal salvation, and those who have not committed their lives to Jesus are forever lost. There is no more opportunity to be saved.

And notice what happens next: chapter 16 says, "Then I heard a loud voice from the temple saying to the seven angels, 'Go, pour out the seven bowls of God's wrath on the earth' " (verse 1). That is precisely the sequence of events that Seventh-day Adventists have always understood with respect to the close of probation and the time of trouble. So the close of probation is clearly a biblical concept. Ellen White simply enlarged upon it.

After the close of probation

When probation closes, all decisions for and against Christ will be final. Those who have put themselves on Christ's side must have made a deliberate, conscious decision to accept Him as Lord and Savior and follow through with a continuous choice to live the Christian life. Those who are against Christ don't need to make a conscious decision to reject Him. All that's necessary is neglect to make a choice *for* Him. And, unfortunately, many people who consider themselves to be good Christians will fall into that camp. These will be the ones who, at Jesus' second coming, will say, "Lord, Lord," and He will say to them, "I never knew you" (Matthew 7:21–23).

What will happen during the time of trouble?

Ellen White describes the time of trouble after the close of probation in great detail in her chapter in *The Great Controversy* titled—appropriately enough—"The Time of Trouble." It mentions three things that will happen during that time.

First, we know that the Holy Spirit will have been completely removed from the wicked. Prior to the close of probation, the Holy Spirit worked among the wicked to draw them to Jesus, but after the close of probation, "the Spirit of God, persistently resisted, has been at last withdrawn."[4] Please note that the Holy Spirit will be withdrawn from the *wicked.* A couple of times over the past several years, I've had people ask me if the Holy Spirit will be withdrawn from God's people after the close of probation. And the answer to that question is *absolutely not!* The only way God's people can obey Him is with the Holy Spirit in their minds and hearts. Furthermore, Paul was very clear that the seal of God is the Holy Spirit (Ephesians 1:13; 4:30).

The second thing to know about the time of trouble is that God's people will wrestle with Him the way Jacob wrestled with the angel (Genesis 32:22–30). And the reason is very simple. Satan will try to persuade them that their cases are hopeless. Ellen White said that

as Satan influenced Esau to march against Jacob, so he will stir up the wicked to destroy God's people in the time of trouble. And as he accused

Jacob, he will urge his accusations against the people of God. . . .

. . . He hopes so to destroy their faith that they will yield to his temptations and turn from their allegiance to God.[5]

This means that God's people will need a very close relationship with Jesus during that time. That's why I've devoted the last chapter of this book to that topic.

The third thing we need to understand during the time of trouble is that sometime in the middle or toward the end of that period, Satan will appear before the world as Christ. Ellen White described this in some detail:

As the crowning act in the great drama of deception, Satan himself will personate Christ. The church has long professed to look to the Saviour's advent as the consummation of her hopes. Now the great deceiver will make it appear that Christ has come. In different parts of the earth, Satan will manifest himself among men as a majestic being of dazzling brightness, resembling the description of the Son of God given by John in the Revelation. Revelation 1:13-15. The glory that surrounds him is unsurpassed by anything that mortal eyes have yet beheld. The shout of triumph rings out upon the air: "Christ has come! Christ has come!" The people prostrate themselves in adoration before him, while he lifts up his hands and pronounces a blessing upon them, as Christ blessed His disciples when He was upon the earth. His voice is soft and subdued, yet full of melody. In gentle, compassionate tones he presents some of the same gracious, heavenly truths which the Saviour uttered; he heals the diseases of the people, and then, in his assumed character of Christ, he claims to have changed the Sabbath to Sunday, and commands all to hallow the day which he has blessed. He declares that those who persist in keeping holy the seventh day are blaspheming his name by refusing to listen to his angels sent to them with light and truth. This is the strong, almost overmastering delusion. . . .

But the people of God will not be misled. The teachings of this false Christ are not in accordance with the Scriptures. His blessing is pronounced upon the worshipers of the beast and his image, the very class upon whom the Bible declares that God's unmingled wrath shall be poured out.[6]

The pressure will be so severe that the fate of God's people will seem hopeless. Some will be thrust into prison; others will find hiding places among the rocks and the mountains. The wicked will be seeking them out to destroy them. Ellen White describes the scene. "To human sight it will appear that the people of God must soon seal their testimony with their blood as did the martyrs before them."[7] "A general decree [will fix] the time when commandment keepers may be put to death."[8]

Then comes their deliverance. The scene changes radically: "With shouts of triumph, jeering, and imprecation, throngs of evil men are about to rush upon their prey, when, lo, a dense blackness, deeper than the darkness of the night, falls upon the earth. Then a rainbow, shining with the glory from the throne of God, spans the heavens and seems to encircle each praying company. The angry multitudes are suddenly arrested. Their mocking cries die away. The objects of their murderous rage are forgotten. With fearful forebodings they gaze upon the symbol of God's covenant and long to be shielded from its overpowering brightness."[9]

During this time, God's people will have the assurance that Jesus Christ is on His way to deliver His chosen people! This is something God's people can truly expect during the time of trouble. It's the one thing that will give them the courage to hang on!

---

1. Francis D. Nichol, ed., *The Seventh-day Adventist Bible Commentary* (Washington, DC: Review and Herald®, 1957), 7:820.

2. Ellen G. White, *The Great Controversy* (Mountian View, CA: Pacific Press®, 1950), 608, 609.

3. White, 618.

4. White, 614.

5. White, 618, 619.

6. White, 624, 625.

7. White, 630.

8. White, 631.

9. White, 635, 636.

Chapter 19

HOW TO PREPARE FOR
THE FINAL CRISIS–PART 2

I pointed out in the previous chapter that preparation for the final crisis involves three things: (1) understanding the details of what will happen during that time, (2) understanding the Seventh-day Adventist mission during that time, and (3) developing a relationship with Jesus that can see us through that difficult time. Understanding the details of what will happen means having a realistic expectation of the events that will take place, and understanding our mission is about the role that God's people are to play during that period. In this chapter, we'll discuss how to prepare spiritually for what lies ahead.

Through the Bible and Ellen White, God has given His prophets much more advance information about the world's final crisis and Christ's second advent than He gave His people prior to the first advent of the Messiah. And the reason is that the main burden at Jesus' first advent rested on Jesus Himself. He's the One who had to conquer Satan and suffer on the cross to bear our sins. But during the final crisis, the main burden rests on God's people. It was especially important for Jesus to have a clear understanding of His mission 2,000 years ago. Today it's especially important for us, His people, to have a clear understanding of the final crisis that we will go through. In this chapter, I will discuss the spiritual preparation that you and I will need in order to be ready for the final crisis and the time of trouble that lies ahead in our day. In order to make this preparation, we must have a clear understanding of three factors: justification, sanctification, and sinlessness. So let's get started.

Justification

At first glance, you may wonder why justification is an important preparation for the final crisis and the time of trouble. After all, justification is the very first step in the salvation process, so that should be a very settled issue by the time God's people reach the final months and years of this world's history. However, it will be extremely important for you and me to understand the biblical teaching about justification during the time of trouble.

It's easy to *think* that we're on God's side in our spiritual life when we aren't. Jesus warned us that when He returns to this earth to take His redeemed people home with Him, some will discover that the preparation they *thought* they had made was inadequate. They will protest, "Lord, Lord, did we not prophesy in your name and in your name drive out demons and in your name perform many miracles?" And Jesus will reply, "I never knew you. Away from me, you evildoers!" (Matthew 7:22, 23). These people *thought* they had a relationship with Jesus; they *thought* they had been justified and sanctified when they hadn't. So I will explain justification briefly, and then we'll discuss sanctification and perfection (or sinlessness).

Justification means that God *counts* us as righteous even though we are sinful people, and we will continue to have a sinful nature until Jesus returns and changes us from being perishable to being imperishable and from mortal to immortal (see 1 Corinthians 15:53, 54). Paul defined justification as "the righteousness of God apart from the law" (Romans 3:21, NKJV), and in her book *Steps to Christ* Ellen White gave a more expanded explanation: "[Christ] lived a sinless life. He died for us, and now He offers to take our sins and give us His righteousness. If you give yourself to Him, and accept Him as your Saviour, then, sinful as your life may have been, for His sake you are accounted righteous. Christ's character stands in place of your character, and you are accepted before God just as if you had not sinned."[1]

Justification and conversion happen simultaneously, and together, they are the first step in the salvation process. So you may be wondering why justification is so important as a preparation for the final crisis and the time of trouble. Isn't sanctification the most important preparation? Sanctification is indeed very important, but a comment by Ellen White in the chapter "The Time of Trouble" in her book *The Great Controversy* explains why justification is also a part of the preparation we need to make for the time of trouble:

> As Satan accuses the people of God on account of their sins, the Lord permits him to try them to the uttermost. Their confidence in God, their faith and firmness, will be severely tested. As they review the past, their hopes sink; for in their whole lives they can see little good. They are fully conscious of their weakness and unworthiness. Satan endeavors to terrify them with the thought that their cases are hopeless, that the stain of their defilement will never be washed away. He hopes so to destroy their faith that they will yield to his temptations and turn from their allegiance to God.[2]

In this situation, it will be critical for God's people to understand that their perfection does not lie within themselves. Their perfection rests with Jesus. *His* righteousness has covered their sinfulness, and they are justified. They are "accepted before God just as if [they] had not sinned."[3] That's why it will be so important during the time of trouble for God's people to have a firm understanding of the biblical teaching about justification and its application to their own lives at that time. *Of course*, they can see little good in their past lives! But their righteousness during the time of trouble will be the same as it was before probation closed: Christ's righteousness standing in place of their sinfulness. Justification is what will give them the courage to persevere and not give up.

Sanctification

God's people who live during the final crisis both before and after the close of probation will also need a very high level of character development. John, in Revelation, described them as 144,000 people who are sealed. Whether this number is to be understood literally or symbolically doesn't matter for the purpose of this discussion. The point is that they have received God's seal on their foreheads.

In Bible times people sealed up documents in much the same way that we seal envelopes today. We have glue on the flap edge of an envelope that we can moisten with our tongues, and when we close it, it's sealed, and it can only be opened by tearing the envelope. In Bible times, the seal was one or more drops of wax placed along the edge of a scroll after it had been rolled up. Thus, the recipient of a document both then and now can be certain that it has not been tampered with as long as the seal on the edge of the scroll or the flap of the envelop has not been broken or torn. Similarly, the seal placed on the foreheads of the 144,000 means that their characters are closed up, and they are assured of salvation in God's kingdom.

In Ephesians 1:13 and 4:30, Paul described God's seal as the Holy Spirit. The most intelligent part of the human brain lies immediately behind the bone of the forehead, so the fact that the 144,000 have the seal of God placed on their foreheads means that God's Holy Spirit has been placed permanently in their minds.

The question then becomes how to obtain God's seal in our minds. There are two answers to that question. The seal of God that Paul describes in the two verses in Ephesians is different from the seal that's placed on the foreheads of the 144,000. In Ephesians 4:30, Paul said, "Do not grieve the Holy Spirit of God, with whom you were sealed for the day of redemption," which suggests that this seal can be revoked or terminated, depending on the decision of the believer. After all, nobody prior to the close of probation is beyond choosing to reject his or her commitment to Jesus. The seal of God on the minds of the 144,000 involves the Holy Spirit, and it's permanent. It prepares them to stand through the great time of trouble after the close of probation. This is evident from the fact that they are sealed prior to the blowing of the four winds, which are a symbol of the great time of trouble. God's seal prepares them to stand through that critical period. And in Revelation 14:1–3, the same 144,000 are in heaven standing before God's throne singing a song that only they can learn.

There have been numerous suggestions as to who these 144,000 are. I believe they are God's people who will pass through the time of trouble, and there's biblical evidence to support this conclusion. Revelation 7:9–17 describes a great multitude of the redeemed who stand before God's throne, and when John asks an elder who this great multitude is his angel interpreter says, "These are they who have come out of the great tribulation" (verse 14). Those are the 144,000, who were sealed immediately before the close of probation and the time of trouble to prepare them to stand through that challenging time.

Will the 144,000 be sinless?

Some Adventists have suggested that the seal of God on the foreheads of the 144,000 will render them sinlessly perfect, and a couple of Ellen White's comments seem to suggest this. The first one I'll share with you comes from the chapter in *The Great Controversy* titled, "The Time of Trouble":

> Now, while our great High Priest is making the atonement for us, we should seek to become perfect in Christ. Not even by a thought could our Saviour be brought to yield to the power of temptation. Satan finds in human hearts some point where he can gain a foothold; some sinful desire is cherished, by means of which his temptations assert their power. But Christ declared of Himself: "The prince of this world cometh, and hath nothing in Me." John 14:30. Satan could find nothing in the Son of God that would enable him to gain the victory. He had kept His Father's commandments, and there was no sin in Him that Satan could use to his advantage. *This is the condition in which those must be found who shall stand in the time of trouble.*[4]

I dealt at some length with this statement in my book, *The 144,000*, which was published by Pacific Press in 2020, and here I will share with you some of the thoughts that I expressed there. I pointed out in that book that Ellen White made a statement in *The Desire of Ages* that is very similar, yet it has some significant differences. Here is her statement in *The Desire of Ages:*

"The prince of this world cometh," said Jesus, "and hath nothing in Me." John 14:30. There was in Him nothing that responded to Satan's sophistry. He did not consent to sin. Not even by a thought did He yield to temptation. So it may be with us. Christ's humanity was united with divinity; He was fitted for the conflict by the indwelling of the Holy Spirit. And He came to make us partakers of the divine nature. So long as we are united to Him by faith, sin has no more dominion over us. God reaches for the hand of faith in us to direct it to lay fast hold upon the divinity of Christ, that we may attain to perfection of character.[5]

Notice one short sentence: "He [Jesus] did not consent to sin," which does not appear in *The Great Controversy* version of the statement. Two sentences later, she said, "So it may be with us." Ellen White did not live during the time of trouble after the close of probation, nor do you and I. So when she said, "So it may be with us," she was talking about the possibility of her and us today living in harmony with her comment about Jesus' perfect life. While her statement in *The Great Controversy* is in the chapter on "The Time of Trouble," the fact that she said almost the very same thing in *The Desire of Ages* is a clear indication that she did not have in mind that we can live like Jesus exclusively in the time of trouble.

Another statement by Ellen White that some Adventists take to mean that God's people will be sinless during the time of trouble is found in her book, *Christ's Object Lessons*: "When the character of Christ shall be perfectly reproduced in His people, then He will come to claim them as His own."[6]

The first thing I will point out is that it would be impossible for you and me to experience Christ's high level of character perfection. He was sinless from the moment He was born until He took His last breath on the cross. No other human being ever has or ever will achieve that level of perfection. I will remind you of the Ellen White statement from page 62 of *Steps to Christ* that I quoted a moment ago: "Christ's character stands in place of your character, and you are accepted before God just as if you had not sinned." Our complete perfection will always be found in Christ's character that He attributes to us, never through our own achievements, even with His divine help.

Finally, I will call your attention to one other statement by Ellen White in her book *The Great Controversy*. This one is also in her chapter "The Time of Trouble." On page 621 she said, "God's love for His children during the period of their severest trial is as strong and tender as in the days of their sunniest prosperity; but it is needful for them to be placed in the furnace of fire; their earthliness must be consumed, that the image of Christ may be perfectly reflected."[7]

The issue here is the definition of the word *earthliness*. Does it mean sinfulness? In my book, *The 144,000*, I referred to three comments by Ellen White that indicate conclusively that earthliness includes sinfulness. While she used the word *earthliness* in a number of other parts of her extensive writings, these three instances, especially the last one, make it very clear that by earthliness she did mean sinfulness:

- "Trial is part of the education given in the school of Christ, to purify God's children from the dross of earthliness."[8]
- "The dust of selfishness and earthliness must be expelled."[9]
- "The Lord permits trials in order that we may be cleansed from earthliness, from selfishness, from harsh, unchristlike traits of character."[10]

Please note that in the third quote, Ellen White used "earthliness" and "unchristlike traits of character" as synonyms. Based on these statements, especially the third one, I have to conclude that some form of sinfulness will remain to be removed from God's people during the time of trouble. Thus, we cannot define sinlessness after the close of probation and during the time of trouble as the total removal of all our character defects, all of our propensities and tendencies to sin.

Finally, I will share with you a brief quotation—just one sentence by Ellen White in which she told us when we *will* have a right to claim to be sinless. She said, "We cannot say, 'I am sinless,' till this vile body is changed and fashioned like unto His glorious body."[11] This agrees with what the apostle John said in 1 John 1:8: "If we claim to be without sin, we deceive ourselves and the truth is not in us."

Anticipating the final crisis and the time of trouble

The final days of this earth's history will be profoundly difficult for God's people. We have a right to expect that. We *need* to expect that. And that expectation needs to motivate us to spend time every day, right now—I suggest at least an hour—in devotional time preparing for the final crisis and the time of trouble. It also needs to motivate us to get on with the mission of God's people in these final days of earth's history, winning people to Jesus and doing our best to prepare both them and ourselves for what we know lies ahead. As you know, awareness of what lies ahead can be frightening. We need to do what the one-talent man failed to do: ask God to help us deal with the fear that can so easily overwhelm us as we reflect on the final crisis and the time of trouble.

My final bit of advice as we come to the end of this book is this: Keep your eyes on Jesus. Trust Him to see you through.

1. Ellen G. White, *Steps to Christ* (Nampa, ID: Pacific Press®, 2003), 62.
2. Ellen G. White, *The Great Controversy* (Mountian View, CA: Pacific Press®, 1950), 618, 619.
3. White, *Steps to Christ*, 62.
4. White, *The Great Controversy*, 623; emphasis added.
5. Ellen G. White, *The Desire of Ages* (Mountian View, CA: Pacific Press®, 1940), 123.
6. Ellen G. White, *Christ's Object Lessons* (Washington, DC: Review and Herald®, 1941), 69.
7. White, *The Great Controversy*, 621.
8. Ellen G. White, *The Acts of the Apostles* (Mountain View, CA: Pacific Press®, 1911), 524.
9. Ellen G. White, *Child Guidance* (Nashville, TN: Southern Publishing, 1954), 497.
10. White, *Christ's Object Lessons*, 175.
11. Ellen G. White, *Selected Messages*, book 3 (Washington, DC: Review and Herald®, 1980), 355.